Maureen Attwooll was educated at Weymouth Grammar School. She is on the staff of Dorset County Library and has worked at Weymouth Library for a number of years. She is one of the acknowledged experts on Weymouth's history and has written widely about the town and its past. Together with Jack West she is the co-author of *Seaside Weymouth* and the definitive history of the town, *Weymouth, An Illustrated History.*

Denise Harrison was born and brought up on Portland and now lives in Weymouth. She has worked in local government, public relations and as a freelance journalist. She is particularly interested in the 1940s and, together with Maureen Attwooll, has spent the last eighteen months researching and writing *Weymouth & Portland at War, Countdown to D-Day.*

Following page
Weymouth Harbour in the summer of 1939. The GWR
vessels and Cosens paddle steamers were soon to be
requisitioned for war service, and the piers and
theatres later came under military control.

WEYMOUTH AND PORTLAND AT WAR

Countdown to D-Day

Maureen Attwooll & Denise Harrison

Maureen Attwooll

Denise Harrison

THE DOVECOTE PRESS

This book is dedicated to all the people of Weymouth and Portland
— men, women and children — and to the American servicemen
and women who passed through Weymouth and Portland,
who lost their lives during the Second World War.

Weymouth beach in August 1939. By the end of the following summer Britain
was threatened by a German invasion and the bathing tents, refreshment kiosks
and deckchairs had been replaced by the paraphernalia of war — barbed wire
entanglements and concrete tank traps.

First published in 1993 by The Dovecote Press Ltd
Stanbridge, Wimborne, Dorset BH21 4JD

ISBN 1 874336 16 4

© Maureen Attwooll and Denise Harrison 1993

Photoset in Palatino by The Typesetting Bureau
Wimborne, Dorset
Printed and bound in Singapore

Contents

Weymouth in the 1930s.

Acknowledgements

Much of this book is based on the personal recollections of people who lived in the Weymouth and Portland area during the war years. The authors are grateful to all those who spared the time to recall their memories of that tumultuous era. One of the most extraordinary discoveries in researching and writing this book has been that there are many people whom we see almost daily, and who appear to lead ordinary and uneventful lives, but who have some incredible stories to tell about their wartime experiences. Some of these tales are funny and some tragic – but all in their own way are heroic.

We would particularly like to thank John and Poppy Butcher for their seemingly endless knowledge of the period, Dawn Gould – a mine of information, Dick Abbott, Dick Bellingham, Graham Coleman, Emily Collins, Wally Dennis, Doris Dowdney, Herbert Klug, Herbert 'Boy' Male, John McComas, Caroline Milverton, Austin Prosser, Bob and Mary Shipman, Peggy Stewkesbury, Mervyn Stewkesbury, John Stone, Harold Thomas, Eric Westmacott, Ken and Mary Weyrauch, the United States Army – and our families for their help and patience.

For permission to quote from *Images of War* by Robert Capa and *By-line: Ernest Hemingway*, we would like to thank the publishers Hamlyn and Collins respectively.

For assistance in providing illustrations we gratefully acknowledge Aerofilms Pictorial Ltd, Geoffrey Carter, Graham Coleman, Dorset County Library, Dorset Evening Echo, Terry Gale, Imperial War Museum, Bill Macey, Stuart Morris, Roger Nailer, Geoff Pritchard, Eva Symes, George Symes, the United States Army, Jack West, Weymouth and Portland Borough Council.

We owe a particular debt of gratitude to the late D.G.F.Acutt, whose book *Brigade in Action*: 'the history of the origin and development of the St John Ambulance Brigade in Weymouth, and its co-operation with the Civil Defence Services during the War, 1939-1945' (published in 1946) is the most detailed illustrated contemporary record of the events of the Second World War in the local area.

We would finally like to thank Harvey G. Bailey of Weymouth and Portland Borough Council for encouraging us to write this book, and our publisher, David Burnett, for his help and advice in its preparation.

MAUREEN ATTWOOLL & DENISE HARRISON
Weymouth, 1993

ONE

Storm Clouds

"Once again the nations are piling up armaments until each land becomes a vast arsenal. Every land echoes to the tramp of training men. Every nation is afraid of its neighbour . . ."
Dorset Daily Echo
11 November 1938

On November 11th 1938 in cities, towns and villages all over Britain, people gathered for the customary Armistice Day services, held to commemorate the end of the Great War, "the war to end all war", twenty years earlier. But as they stood for the traditional two-minute silence, the thoughts of many must surely have strayed to the events of a few weeks before, when Prime Minister Neville Chamberlain had returned from meeting the German Chancellor, Adolf Hitler, in Munich to announce that he had secured "peace in our time".

Few believed the Prime Minister. War with Germany had been expected since the mid-1930's, the decade which had seen the swift and ruthless rise to power of Adolf Hitler and the Nazi Party, with the German dictator openly flouting the conditions of the Treaty of Versailles, the peace agreement imposed on Germany in 1919. The terms of Versailles had stripped the country economically, militarily and territorily and its hopes of recovery were dashed in the worldwide Great Depression of the Thirties. Hitler's powers of oratory convinced a huge following that a new German empire – the Third Reich – could be created. As its leader, or Fuhrer, he held absolute power and set about eradicating civil and political rights, started the systematic persecution of the Jews, reintroduced conscription and began re-arming Germany. As other nations watched, protested, but did not act, he looked beyond German borders seeking to enlarge his territory.

Left: An alas slightly faded aerial photograph of Weymouth Sands during the August Bank Holiday weekend, 1938.

In March 1936, Hitler's troops re-occupied the Rhineland, an area between France and Germany demilitarised at Versailles, and early in 1938 the German Army successfully invaded Austria. In September the Munich Crisis was precipitated by Hitler laying claim to the German-speaking Sudetenland, an important industrial region of Czechoslovakia. Despite Czech protests, the policy of appeasing Germany continued and the Sudetenland was handed over after Hitler promised that this would be his last territorial claim in Europe. Six months later his troops occupied the rest of Czechoslovakia.

By the time war was declared on the 3rd September 1939, it came as no surprise. Two days earlier, Hitler's forces had invaded Poland – and their immediate withdrawal was demanded by Britain and France. The British ultimatum expired at 11 am and, as it did so, on that autumn Sunday morning, Neville Chamberlain's voice was heard on wireless sets across the nation:

"I am speaking to you from the Cabinet Room at No. 10 Downing Street. This morning, the British Ambassador in Berlin handed the German government a final note stating that unless the British government heard from them by 11 o'clock that they were prepared to withdraw their troops from Poland, a state of war would exist between us. I have to tell you now that no such undertaking has been received, and that consequently this country is at war with Germany . . ."

One Portlander remembers :

"We had never believed Hitler and his promises, even when Chamberlain came back waving his bit of paper! We knew we would have to go to war".

The newest attraction on Weymouth seafront in the summer of 1939 was the Pier Bandstand, shown here in this aerial photograph.

A Weymouth man – aged 13 at the time – reacted with excited anticipation:

"I thought – we all thought – that we would make short work of Adolf Hitler!"

War came to Weymouth at a time when the town was at the height of its fame as a traditional English seaside resort. The bleak years which had followed the end of World War I were long gone and, despite the Depression of the Thirties, holidaymakers poured into the town by the thousand, arriving by train, motor coach and car.

If the beach attractions of sailing, swimming, sandcastle-building and Punch and Judy began to pall, there were excursions aplenty to beauty spots in the surrounding countryside. Charabancs, hoods down on a sunny day, lined up on the open space in front of the King's Statue, ready to take trippers to Sutton Poyntz, Upwey Wishing Well and a host of other popular venues, usually with a strawberry or cream tea en route. A trip to Portland was also a must, and the Island could be reached by steamer or via the scenic route of the Weymouth and Portland Railway. Either way, there was a chance to see some of the Royal Navy's latest warships in Portland Harbour, vessels of the Home Fleet being regular visitors.

Evening and wet weather entertainment was provided by four cinemas in the town, with a further two on Portland, several dance halls and two theatres – The Pavilion on the pier, and the Alexandra Gardens Theatre close by. At the opposite end of the Esplanade the Pier Bandstand opened in 1939, in Art Deco style and with the latest in neon lighting. The Bandstand hosted heats of the Miss Weymouth competition in the afternoons and open-air ballroom dancing on balmy summer evenings.

Although tourism was undoubtedly Weymouth's main industry, another major source of employment was the Harbour, with all its associated trades. The Great Western Railway's steamers ran a daily service to Guernsey and Jersey in the summer months (thrice weekly in winter) and the quay bustled with cargo trade. Depending on the season, crate after crate of potatoes, cauliflowers, tomatoes and flowers were unloaded and sent on their way inland. The skyline was regularly dominated by the tall masts of graceful sailing ships from the Baltic, bringing timber into the port. Cosens and Company operated pleasure steamer trips in local waters as well as running excursion boats farther afield to other seaside resorts such as Swanage, Bournemouth and Torquay. The company, who were long-established marine engineers, also carried out salvage work and repairs. Another feature of Weymouth Harbour, the lifeboat *William and Clara Ryland*, was one of the most up-to-date in service at the time.

Boundary extensions in 1933 had brought the surrounding villages into the Borough and the town's population at the end of the 1930s numbered around 30,000. Other employers of sizeable workforces were Portland Naval Base and Dockyard, Whiteheads Torpedo Works at Wyke Regis, the two breweries in Hope Square and the usual service industries.

Portland's residents numbered around 12,000 and although considered as one unit from a military point of view during World War II, Weymouth and Portland were quite separately administered in local government terms. The Island's main industry was the quarrying of its famous stone and the skilled carving done by local stone masons decorated many world-famous buildings. For the men working in the quarries there were plenty of reminders of World War I. The Whitehall Cenotaph was cut from stone taken from a specially-opened quarry and Portland also provided more than half-a-million memorial slabs commemorating the fallen on the Western Front.

At Castletown, the naval base's importance had increased in 1924 with the establishment of the shore based HMS *Osprey*, headquarters in the UK of all secret anti-submarine warfare research and development. Visiting "bluejackets" from Royal Navy ships regularly disembarked from liberty boats at Weymouth Pier, mingling with the holiday crowds and swelling the takings at the local pubs.

No wonder the speeches of South Dorset MP Lord Cranborne fell largely on deaf ears as he toured his constituency warning of the coming Nazi menace.

During the summer of 1936, among the sideshows and barrel organs on Weymouth Sands, a Numerologist entertained the holidaymakers. By adding up dates of previous wars, he predicted – to the amusement of the crowd – that there was soon to be another war and that it would break out in 1939.

Getting Ready

The protection of the civilian population in time of war was being considered as early as 1935, when, following Home Office guidelines, Weymouth tentatively set up the Air Raid Precautions Committee. Its members began discussing a range of possible war situations which later became all too real, from the distribution of gas masks and restrictions on lighting to the treatment of casualties and removal of unexploded bombs.

Trained volunteers would be needed if war broke out and late in 1937 some two hundred people turned up at a public meeting in Weymouth Guildhall to find out what being an Air Raid Warden was all about. ARP posts were established and training began. It was fairly casual at first, no-one else took them very seriously and one warden recalled that they were looked on as "slightly odd", laden with wooden gas rattles, first aid kits, hooded flashlights, handbells to sound the "all clear" and a steel helmet. Portland, too, was training its first ARP recruits.

Following the Munich Crisis in September 1938 an appeal for more Civil Defence volunteers went out – a call which was to be repeated again and again during the early stages of the war. By the end of September, First Aid Posts were being set up and instructions were issued to the St John Ambulance ARP Casualty Service on procedures to be followed if air raid sirens sounded. Car and van owners were asked to volunteer their vehicles to supplement the town's two ambulances and the ARP Committee drew up a list of commercial vehicles which could be called on in an emergency. Early in 1939 a National Service Bureau opened at the Employment Exchange in St Thomas Street. As well as recruiting for the regular and reserve forces it had vacancies in the ARP, Auxiliary Fire Service, Special Constabulary, Nursing and First Aid, Rescue and Decontamination Squads and a host of others. Over the winter months there had been a change of emphasis – the talk of "*if* war breaks out" had become "*when* war breaks out".

In April 1939 a full-time ARP Officer was appointed and the following month, Weymouth's Medical Officer of Health, Dr E J Gordon Wallace, was made responsible for all casualty services in the area (the doctor received his call-up papers in August, but fortunately for the town the War Office looked favourably on an application for him to

The first big test of ARP efficiency in April 1939.

In a dilapidated house opposite the Old Borough Arms in Chickerell Road, gas-masked members of the rescue services participate in the practice 'black-out' of April 1939.

Mayor J.T. 'Joe' Goddard had no idea when he appealed for volunteers to assist in transporting evacuees billeted in Weymouth that it would be one of many such appeals, or that his one-year term of office would be extended until 1945.

remain in the borough).

At the end of April the first full-scale mock battle and blackout exercise took place in South Dorset. ARP personnel were mobilised, communications systems tested and air raid sirens tried out (church bells were tolled to alert those in villages without sirens). It was a major training exercise, and the first that brought home the difficulty of coping with

AN AIR RAID REFUGE ROOM IN YOUR HOME

This Plan tells you how to fit one up

By May 1938 war seemed inevitable, leading to the town's Air Raid Precautions Committee issuing this plan of how best to prepare your own home against an air raid.

emergency situations in pitch darkness. Another blackout test was carried out early in July. To ensure that the area was not visible to enemy pilots during darkness windows of every building had to be completely obscured. Shops quickly ran out of the thick "blackout" curtain material sold for the purpose. Temporary makeshift shutters of black card pinned to wooden battens soon wore out in wartime and recipes for a thick, black and very messy dye for treating other materials began to appear.

Despite worsening news from Europe, a stepping-up of emergency measures at home and the certainty that the actual outbreak of hostilities was close, there was a determined gaiety about the Bank Holiday Weekend at the beginning of August.

Incoming trains were packed and traffic queued bumper to bumper along Weymouth seafront. Holidaymakers sent off 100,000 picture postcards, flocked to Val Vaux's Vaudeville Theatre on the sands and enjoyed Billy Cotton's Band at the Alexandra Gardens Theatre. Highlight of the coming week, and so close it was almost an extension of the Bank Holiday, was the visit of King George VI to review the Reserve Fleet assembled in Weymouth Bay. Visitors watched 133 ships at anchor being made spick and span for the Royal inspection on August 9th, when there was a further influx of day trippers.

The crowds were such that the waiting room and later the parcels office at Weymouth Station became

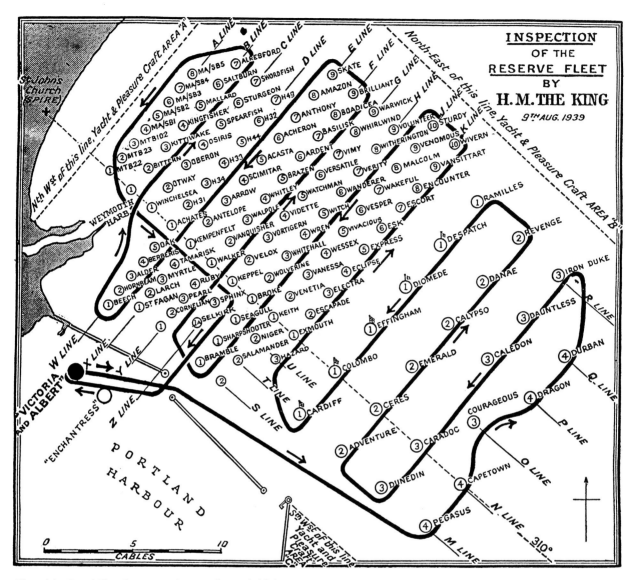

Plan of the Royal Fleet Review in Weymouth Bay, held three weeks before war broke out. 133 ships took part in the Review, which as well as motor torpedo boats, trawlers, and tugs included four cruiser squadrons, 50 destroyers, the aircraft carrier *Courageous* and three great battleships, *Revenge, Ramillies,* and *Iron Duke.* The thick black line shows the route taken by the royal yacht.

a makeshift casualty clearing station, so great were the numbers who fainted.

In damp fog, pleasure boats from the pier and beach ran trips to view the impressive armada, ranged in lines across Weymouth Bay. In the Royal Yacht *Victoria and Albert* the King reviewed the Fleet, which included the battleships *Ramillies, Revenge*

and *Iron Duke.* Even as the King left Weymouth that evening, the ships were preparing to sail to their war stations. Some 42 were later to be lost in enemy action, the Aircraft Carrier *Courageous* in less than six weeks.

It was the King's second visit to Weymouth that summer. On July 21st, accompanied by the Queen

A cartoon from *Punch* of the Royal Fleet Review. The caption was headed 'NEPTUNE IN WEYMOUTH BAY' and read, 'All's well Girls. You can go on playing'.

Volunteer now! A recruiting display for the local casualty services early in 1939.

and the Princesses Elizabeth and Margaret he had arrived by train to join the Royal Yacht en route for Dartmouth. He was to make a third trip at the end of September, but there were no cheering crowds. War had broken out, and the morale-boosting visit "to troops in the south-west of England" was surrounded in secrecy for security reasons. War had brought press censorship into force. From now on any hint of military activity in the Weymouth and Portland area which might assist the enemy was reported as occurring in "a well known south coast town", recognisable to those who lived here but, hopefully, not to the Germans.

War preparations continued throughout the summer. One of the greatest fears was that the country might be subjected to attacks of poison gas, in part a legacy of the First World War when mustard gas had been used with such horrific consequences in the trenches. Anti-gas lectures were held, decontamination centres established and gas masks arrived — 34,000 for Weymouth and a further 11,000 for Portland, enough to fit everyone except the smallest

babies. Volunteer squads assembled the masks at amazing speed and they were distributed to various depots in the area for collection by the public during August. The masks were fitted and tested in a "testing chamber", although the testing method for civilian respirators was more likely to be "You put your hand over the filter — if you couldn't suck air in, it was OK"! Most people hated putting them on because of the claustrophobic feeling and the "awful smell of rubber".

That same month the local weekly newspaper office reported good sales of its instruction leaflet and diagram entitled "How to fit up an air raid refuge in your home". Articles followed on the recognition of enemy aircraft, accompanied by silhouette drawings.

Reservists were called up : the ARP was mobilised. From the 1st September full blackout was enforced from dusk until dawn when streetlights were off, car headlights masked, and windows and doors made absolutely "light-tight". Air Raid Wardens checked for violations against the blackout regulations and the cry of "Put that light out!" became all too

A good crowd gathers to watch a pre-war demonstration by
the gas decontamination squad in the car park alongside
Westham Bridge. The Arts Centre and Jubilee Hall can be seen
in the background.

familiar. Although kerbs and posts had been painted
white to be visible in dark streets, the intense
blackness took some getting used to, and many a
local found himself lost within yards of his own
front door. Weymouth Harbour proved a particular
hazard, particularly for those coming out of the
quayside pubs, as did the sharp bends on Portland's
roads. The lighting restrictions caused the cancella-
tion until the end of the war of both Portland's
colourful Pleasure Fair and Weymouth's traditional
seafront Guy Fawkes bonfires and fireworks.

Weymouth Station was again the focus for the
emergency services when, on the 1st September,
hundreds of apprehensive children evacuated from
London, with some mothers and school teachers,
arrived in the town by special train. Weymouth and
Portland had been designated a "safe place" and
throughout the night and into the following day,

the schools acted as reception and allocation centres
to the evacuees who were found accommodation
with local families. It was the first taste of all-night
duty for the casualty and voluntary services.

The sudden increase of children meant over-
crowded schools having to work to a rota system,
not only to accommodate all the pupils but also to
make evacuation easier in the event of an air raid.
Concentrations of the population were very much at
risk from air attack and schools were particularly
vulnerable, but trench shelters were dug near all
school buildings and autumn term began as usual on
September 18th. Additional air raid precautions
followed later. Most local children were delighted at
having to attend school on a part time basis. At the
Central School in Cromwell Road, the day was split
into three two-hourly shifts.

Wally Dennis, son of a commended SJAB Officer,

composed a poem while a 13-year old at Weymouth Central School – a schoolboy's-eye view of life on the home front!

Your War Effort

We're fighting for justice – a good cause at that
On which the Nazis vainly spat,
But in the end we'll prove them wrong
And show their regime is not so strong.

In our factories we make mines
Guns and tanks of every kind,
Bullets, bombs and aeroplanes large
And bayonets with which our soldiers charge.

In our planes the airmen fly
Shooting the enemy out of the sky,
On bombing raids they also go
Through wind and lightning, hail and snow.

The Army and Navy and others too
Home Guards and Wardens are sticking it through,
First Aiders and Firemen are doing the same
Helping to beat Jerry at his own game.

Many local people suspected that an area with a large naval anchorage would be anything but a "safe place" in wartime. Come 1940 and the first air raids, they were proved right and many of the London children returned home. Billeting surveys had shown the town to be capable of taking 9,000 evacuees – the eventual total was around 6,000, with some 800 on Portland. "Unexpected" arrivals in this first batch were 100 expectant mothers, and numbers 13 and 13a Greenhill were requisitioned and hastily converted to a Maternity Home. Some families accepted incredible numbers of children into their homes. Mrs Price of Abbotsbury Road looked after seventeen London youngsters in addition to her own nine, and Mrs Allan of Verne Road took in sixteen.

Opposite Weymouth Station, in King Street, Christchurch was on the verge of closure (largely through disuse) in 1939. Stripped of its ecclesiastical fittings, the church was converted to a social centre, re-opening in November 1939 as the "Welcome Club" for evacuees. The Jubilee Hall at Portland provided similar facilities. Accustomed to city streets, London children found Dorset a strange and inviting landscape. Despite warnings of its dangers, two Portland evacuees aged 6 and 8 climbed a 16-foot high boulder at Church Ope Cove and fell off the top. They recovered, but a 12-year old boy who slipped down a quarry on the island died of his injuries.

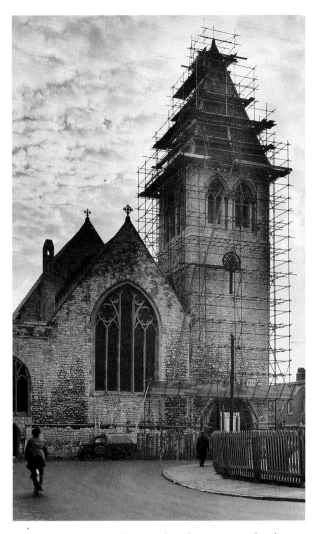

Christchurch, opposite Weymouth Railway Station, shortly before demolition in November 1956. During the war it served as a 'Welcome Club' for evacuees, an emergency feeding centre and a British Restaurant.

Although the news was not unexpected and despite the preparations going on all around them, once it became official that Britain was at war with Germany, people did not know what to expect. Some imagined that enemy aircraft would be overhead within hours, followed by bombs and gas attacks. Others forecast that "it would be all over by Christmas".

In Weymouth a few late holidaymakers helped to fill sandbags on the beach before returning home. In fact there was to be little activity on land during the "Phoney War" as the first months came to be called, but plenty was happening at sea off Dorset's coast.

17

TWO

The Phoney War

As Hitler planned his relentless advance across Northern Europe, the German Navy turned its attention to severing the vital lifelines which brought everything from raw materials to food into Britain by sea. In the first three months of the war the German fleet sank 200,000 tons of Allied shipping.

Enemy action in the Channel began almost at once. German submarines began laying mines to destroy Allied naval and merchant shipping. In the coming months, as Hitler attempted a complete blockade of Britain, shipping in the Channel was also to be subjected to dive bombing raids from the air and deadly attacks by stealthy E-boats, fast German motor torpedo craft.

Portland was vulnerable to attack by sea or air and the defences of the naval base were strengthened. In the years between the wars, Portland Dockyard had grown in importance. It frequently saw ships of the Home Fleet, served as a working up base for Royal Navy vessels of all classes, was a repair facility and an oil storage port. HMS *Osprey* housed the headquarters of anti-submarine warfare in Britain, engaging in vital research work. German aerial photographs which came into British hands after hostilities ended show that the Luftwaffe had made a very thorough survey of Portland and Weymouth harbours in the summer of 1939.

Gun emplacements were hurriedly constructed at various points overlooking the Harbour and Channel. Two 9.2" guns were situated at Blacknor, two 6" guns at the Breakwater Fort, with 12 pounder guns at the Nothe, the Verne, and strategic positions on Portland. At the Breakwater forts, the completion of searchlight installations and living accommodation for troops was accelerated.

In time of war it was necessary to establish an examination service and contraband control to ensure that vessels attempting to enter port were "friendly", and that merchant ships were not carrying cargo likely to assist the enemy's war effort.

Under the Portland command, the examination anchorage was based in Weymouth Bay, with offices in the Edward Hotel. The navy required extra vessels for the work, since up to 50 ships might be awaiting inspection in the Bay. Local craft were pressed into service, including four pleasure steamers from Cosens' fleet – the *Monarch, Victoria, Consul* and *Empress.* In the first four weeks following the outbreak of war 1,000 tons of contraband freight were seized.

All the harbour entrances were sealed before sunset, initially by boom defences. At the height of the invasion scare in 1940 Portland's were to be strengthened by the addition of loaded torpedo tubes, whilst at Weymouth an old cargo ship, the *Kenfig Pool,* was swung across the harbour entrance every night, effectively blocking it.

In the early days of the war, the German Navy's U-Boat U26 was busy laying mines in the Channel off Portland. The area's first experience of hostile action came on the 15th September 1939 when the 5965-ton Belgian steamer *Alex van Opstal*, returning to Antwerp from New York, fell victim to one of these mines five miles east of the Shambles lightship. In rough seas and a northerly wind, the ship broke in two and sank. The 67 survivors were rescued by a Greek vessel and brought ashore at Weymouth. Less than three weeks later, a Dutch merchant vessel was mined in the same area. En route to Rotterdam from New York, the *Binnendijk* had been ordered to change course for Weymouth Bay for a contraband examination. The crew of 42, together with the ship's cat Katie, were taken off the blazing vessel by the examination boat and the *Binnendijk* sank shortly afterwards.

The dangerous Shambles shoal had been marked by buoys and later a lightship for well over one hundred years, but the following summer when German air attacks on shipping in the Channel intensified, the Shambles Lightship itself became a vulnerable target and it was removed until after the war.

With the loss of a further merchant steamship, the *Elena R*, to an enemy mine in November, the St John Ambulance Brigade was asked by the Naval Authorities to form a Naval First Aid Party, prepared to go to sea to attend casualties on stricken vessels in local waters. During the coming year, these First Aiders were called out regularly to treat seamen injured by German mines, bombs and machine gun attack in the Channel. On one occasion, having collected their casualties, the St John Ambulance men had to "sit tight" at sea as bombs and bullets rained down on them from enemy aircraft above. Miraculously, they were able to return to Weymouth Harbour without further injury. The party comprised the Medical Officer, two St John Ambulance Brigade men, and one Nurse. Volunteers for the position of Nurse were invited, the most important qualifications being: "She should not be prone to seasickness, she should be fairly agile, and she should be able to reassure and control women passengers who may be very frightened and hysterical".

But this was neither the time nor the place for women to be faint-hearted. The National Service Campaign of 1939 had resulted in those able-bodied men who were not engaged in reserved occupations enlisting for service, and it would be left to women to roll up their sleeves and take over the jobs they had vacated. At Whitehead's Torpedo Factory, women who had been employed as office staff pre-War were deployed to the factory floor. A popular song of the time went: "And it's the girl that makes the thing, That holds the oil that oils the ring, That works the thingumebob, That's going to Win the War".

The Whitehead Works had been modernised in the 1930s and production increased as a result – in 1939 the factory was turning out some 500 torpedoes a year. All work on foreign contracts ceased on the outbreak of war and everything produced went to the Admiralty. Like other large workplaces in the town, the Works formed its own ARP and Firefighting groups and, later, a sizeable Home Guard Division. Other local firms turned their output over to the war effort – on the opposite side of the road at Ferrybridge W & J Tod's yard stopped building luxury boats and concentrated on motor launches and specialist craft for the Admiralty and Air Ministry. In Weymouth, Cosens' workshops, yards and slipways were put to use repairing a never ending stream of vessels damaged in enemy action, whilst

A Luftwaffe aerial reconnaissance photograph of Portland Harbour taken in the summer of 1939.

on Portland quarry machines and equipment went over to "war work".

Many of the allied shipping losses in these early months of war were caused by a British invention of World War I, subsequently developed by German scientists – the magnetic mine. Capable of being dropped into the sea from aircraft, this lethal weapon rose up and collided with any ship which passed over it. One landed in the Thames Estuary and failed to explode, enabling the Navy to dismantle it and British scientists to develop a foil. At Portland in February 1940, the manufacture of "degaussing cables" designed to reverse the current of the magnetic mine and de-activate it, started. These cables, fitted to ships by Naval personnel, proved so effective that inmates of the Portland Borstal Institution were deployed in their manufacture. By April the Navy had "coiled" 31 ships.

Rationing Begins

The shipping losses meant shortages were inevitable and by early in 1940 everyone had been issued with an Identity Card and a Ration Book containing coupons to be presented when shopping. First to be rationed were bacon, ham and butter at 4 ounces per person per week, the weekly allowance for sugar being 12 ounces. The press urged householders to register with their local shopkeepers. Meat rationing followed in March, and tea in July. Jam, cheese, margarine and sweets, as well as petrol, clothes, material and footwear were to follow over the next two years. The shortage of tea, restricted to 2 ounces per person per week, was the most serious hardship to many and the making of a pot of tea now involved one spoonful for each person and "none for the pot". White bread became a distant memory and was replaced by unbleached brown.

By 1941 it was possible to supplement these meagre rations with an inexpensive no-coupons meal at one of the government-sponsored "British Restaurants" which served simple, filling food in cafeteria-style surroundings. By the end of the war there were two thousand of them throughout the country. Weymouth had four − calling them "Cookery Nooks" − at the Wyke Hotel, Christchurch, the Rock Hotel and the Sidney Hall. Eightpence purchased a meal (joint and two veg. 6d, pudding 2d), soup was 2d extra, and childrens' portions cost less. The restaurants proved invaluable when people were bombed out of their homes as no-one "on rations" had enough food to share.

To ease the food shortage the "Dig for Victory" campaign began in 1939 and all spare land was turned over to food production. Flowerbeds became vegetable plots almost overnight, and the playing field at Broadwey produced a good crop of oats and barley in the first year of the war.

Savings campaigns were organised for practically everything − from money to waste paper. "Savings Weeks" with specific targets in view were later to raise astonishing sums, but initially the emphasis was on saving paper (by 1940 shoppers were being asked to provide their own bags and wrappings) and scrap metal for munitions. Viewed with hindsight these collections proved to be too successful and much that was unique was lost for ever. Dumped on the growing pile of waste paper were Weymouth's 19th century Workhouse records and much local council archive material from Portland. Decorative and architecturally valuable iron railings went to be melted down for munitions and were never re-placed. Another casualty was the historic Russian gun and its carriage, a relic of the Crimean War and long part of the Pier scenery at Weymouth.

The "Phoney War" continued through the winter of 1939-40 and into the early spring. The lull allowed those who were in the Civil Defence forces to step up training and exercises, and gave those who weren't the opportunity to grumble about the ARP wardens being paid to do nothing but boss people about, numbers of the local people having been hauled before the magistrates for infringements of the blackout (the fine was initially 10/- but it was to increase to a maximum of £15 as the war went on).

Air Raid Protection

Although there was as yet no sign of an air attack, provision of air raid protection was a great concern. In the home, a strengthened basement was the safest place to be, but many houses in Weymouth and Portland had no below-ground accommodation. People were advised to stay under staircases, sit under heavy tables, or brace themselves against a ground-floor door frame. Net and tape could be glued to windows to prevent flying splinters during a bomb blast. In the summer the distribution of Anderson Shelters began. These deceptively flimsy-looking curved steel sheets were bolted together to form an arch, which went into a 7'6" by 6' by 4' hole dug deep in the garden. The resulting hump-backed shelter was completed with steel ends and a hole at ground level for access. With a 15" deep layer of earth over its roof, the Anderson was surprisingly strong and withstood most blasts apart from a direct hit. Damp and earthy and designed to hold six people, they frequently held many more and saved countless lives. 1941 was to see the introduction of an indoor shelter − the Morrison − resembling a large steel table with a steel-mattress base and wire mesh sides. These proved invaluable in "tip and run" raids when families had only seconds to get under cover.

Street shelters were provided − brick-built windowless boxes with a concrete slab roof which gave protection from flying glass and debris, but not a direct hit. In one or two areas of the borough where streets were narrow and front gardens non-existent these shelters had to be erected just a couple of feet from the front of the nearest house. Improvisation was often necessary, and the Central School turned their playing fields at the Links into dug-out trenches, pulling covers over themselves once in-

Distribution of Anderson shelters began in the summer of 1940. Not everyone in the Borough had a garden and communal shelters were provided elsewhere.

side. Many looked for ways of providing shelter with the minimum disruption to daily life and business. Weymouth's Clinton Restaurant converted its basement into a shelter where customers could eat undisturbed, and in Portland the landlord of the Star Inn at Fortuneswell cleared his cellar for use by neighbours and customers during red alerts! Growing numbers of military personnel coming into the area in the early months of the war required leisure facilities and in February 1940 Mayor Joe Goddard opened a Services Club in the requisitioned Palladium Cinema on the Town Bridge. Later the same year Mrs Dorothy King of the National British Women's Abstinence League founded another at the St John's Mission Hall in Chelmsford Street. Others followed. These centres, where men and women of the forces could meet, obtain refreshments, write letters, enjoy music or simply relax were much appreciated as the war went on. Staffed by volunteers, they provided a welcome "home from home" for the many who had no idea when they would see their own homes and families again.

By May 1940 invasion fears were heightening in the face of the seemingly unstoppable German advance in Europe. On the 14th May the Secretary of State for War broadcast an appeal for men between the ages of 17 and 65 to "take up arms" and defend their home towns. The response was dramatic and resulted in the formation of one of the largest unpaid armies ever known – the Local Defence Volunteers, renamed the "Home Guard" in July. Boys and men rushed to enlist and the Weymouth & Portland District's 5th Battalion quickly reached a strength of 2000. Their only uniform an armband bearing the initials "LDV", and with makeshift "weapons" of sticks or chair legs (the broadcast had failed to indicate how they were to arm themselves, since all available weapons were in the hands of the regular forces), their role was to defend the area against enemy attack, expected to be by way of parachute drop.

The LDV was soon jokingly said to stand for "Look, Duck and Vanish". Later in the year, as the Home Guard, they would be issued with uniforms and rifles and given proper training in the use of firearms and grenades. Seventeen year-old John Butcher, newly recruited to the Home Guard and not yet issued with a rifle, was given the task of following the marching "troops" on training exercises in Old Wyke with a cobbled- together device of a gas rattle amplified through a megaphone which

John Butcher, aged seventeen, a member of Whitehead's Home Guard. His 1st World War Lee Enfield rifle was issued with a bayonet and 100 rounds of ammunition, which he had to keep at home when not on duty.

alarmingly. His platoon colleagues immersed him in the water of Littlesea, but he and his rescuers sustained serious burns in the process.

Whiteheads Torpedo Works, having fit young men in reserve occupations, formed its own Home Guard, primarily to defend the factory from air, sea and land attacks. The 600-strong unit was armed with ancient Lee Enfield and Ross rifles, a few hand grenades, and petrol bombs – glass bottles filled with petrol, ignited by Swan Vesta matches taped to the side. One of them remembers : "As part of the Vicker's Group, we had the use of the Company's two water-cooled mobile machine guns". In addition, Whiteheads' Home Guard took over the manning of an anti-aircraft gun, nicknamed "Aggie", sited at the Sports Field at Downclose. Dick Abbott recalls that the gun crews formed special firing parties to defend the coastal area against attack.

"The sole duty of the crews was to load and arm one 21" torpedo and one 18" torpedo each night and prepare for firing, and to withdraw these from the tubes the next morning".

The Whiteheads battery was augmented by two French machine guns sited at the Fleet overlooking the Channel and later by four mighty twin mounted Browning anti-aircraft guns at Ferry Bridge, now the site of Chesil Beach Holiday Camp.

Evacuation of Dunkirk

Meanwhile the enemy was on the move. Neutral Denmark and Norway had been invaded in April. On the 10th May the German forces advanced into Belgium, Holland, Luxembourg and France.

Faced with this new crisis Chamberlain was forced to resign, and he was replaced as Prime Minister by the inspirational Winston Churchill firing the British people, who felt deflated with the Phoney War, with a new determination.

It was not a moment too soon. In just two weeks the advance of the German Army brought their forces to the brink of the Channel coast, cutting off the British Expeditionary Force, of which the 2nd Battalion of the Dorsetshire Regiment formed part. They were trapped at Dunkirk. The only way out was by sea and "Operation Dynamo" was set in motion to bring them back. During the last weeks of May and into early June ships from Portland, as well as pleasure boats from Poole and Weymouth, were called to help evacuate Allied troops from the

could be made to sound like a machine gun. His job was to test the battle readiness of colleagues by activating the device when they least expected it!

In less exceptional circumstances it might be thought to be tempting fate to entrust potentially deadly weapons to the hands of young and inexperienced men. One young Home Guard member, carrying a phosphorous anti-tank bomb in his battle dress pocket, threw himself to the ground during training. The glass phial burst and flamed up

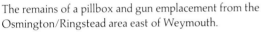
The remains of a pillbox and gun emplacement from the Osmington/Ringstead area east of Weymouth.

beaches of Dunkirk, and later from the ports of northern France.

Weymouth's two long-serving Great Western passenger steamers played a significant part at Dunkirk. Redundant on the suspension of the Weymouth-Channel Islands service in September 1939, both were requisitioned, the *St Julien* being converted for use as a hospital ship. The *St Julien* made several successful runs to Dunkirk and the *St Helier* achieved a remarkable eight crossings, saving 10,200 Allied troops and 15,000 refugees, for which her Captain and First and Second Officers were awarded the DSC, and her Quartermaster the DSM. A cargo service to the Channel Islands was still being maintained at this date, but the GWR's *Roebuck* was pressed into service and saved 600 from the beaches, after which both the *Roebuck* and her sister ship the *Sambur* were requisitioned for war service.

The withdrawal of our troops from the Continent would have further implications for the area when, from the 21st May, 3784 Dutch and Belgian refugees, together with "hundreds of bicycles", were landed at Weymouth Docks from passenger ships, trawlers, and Belgian fishing boats. They had fled their homes in fear of the Luftwaffe's "Blitzkreig", and carried all their possessions with them. As Port Medical Officer, Dr Gordon Wallace was responsible

for the medical inspection and classification of these exhausted and bewildered aliens. Using a system of coloured ribbon, stretcher cases, expectant mothers and infectious patients were despatched to the appropriate hospital, while "verminous" patients were removed to the Cleansing Station in the Corporation Yard. All others were given a white ribbon and sent to the Alexandra Gardens – in use as a reception centre and dining hall – where they were fed and given food parcels for their onward journey. Later in the day many were put on special trains at Weymouth Quay, whilst others were billeted overnight at the Alexandra Hall, the Regent Dance Hall, or local schools.

Between the final weeks of May and the 18th June, Weymouth was to receive thousands of refugees on an almost daily basis, including 10,000 Free French and Moroccan soldiers who had been lifted from the coast of France. Battle-racked and possessing only the clothes they wore, they were to recuperate and re-assemble before being returned to France to fight again. The immediate dilemma for the Weymouth authorities was where to put them, but once again the local organisations and townspeople rallied round. Thousands of residents responded to an appeal from the Town Clerk to provide temporary accommodation, and delighted local children again went uneducated as schools were closed to be used as billets, the ever-resourceful teachers acting as interpreters. The Welcome Club at Christchurch in King Street served up bread and tinned "bully-beef" to the troops, and their departure two days later was to rueful farewells from the locals who had taken the sad and weary soldiers to their hearts.

June also saw the evacuation of the Channel Islands under the shadow of German invasion, as over 23,000 Islanders passed through Weymouth — bearing baskets of tomatoes which they had refused to abandon for the enjoyment of the enemy! Within days, Weymouth temporarily hosted a further 3,531 refugees from continental war zones, making an astonishing total for that week of 27,400. The safe passage into the port of Weymouth of such vast numbers was something of an achievement, as German E and U-Boats constantly harried shipping in the Channel off Portland, and during June several vessels fell victim to enemy mines.

War Zone

The early summer of 1940 then witnessed the transformation of an area usually bustling with holidaymakers. Weymouth and Portland became part of a proclaimed war zone which extended along the coast and for twenty miles inland. Coils of barbed wire replaced deck chairs along the deserted beaches and Esplanade, anti-tank obstacles and pill boxes straddled Chesil Beach, and the grim muzzles of anti-aircraft guns were aimed at waters which had

hitherto been the domain of pleasure craft and bathers. Familiar areas were now "out of bounds". The "south coast town" of the censored war reporting became truly anonymous as place names were obliterated from signposts, railway stations, monuments and plaques. The sweetshop signs for "Weymouth Rock" had to go and posters advertising local events were taken down.

Movement within the zone was restricted and Identity Cards were to be carried at all times. A special permit — or a valid reason — was required for entering the area. The locals, used to welcoming tourists at that time of year, became suspicious of strangers and ever-anxious of enemy infiltration. Slogans such as "Careless Talk Costs Lives", which had seemed a bit of a joke in the early days of the war, were now not so funny.

Some families of those serving in the Royal Navy had already received news of fathers, husbands or sons being killed, captured, or missing, and the surrender of France on the 22nd June, followed by the occupation of the Channel Islands on the 30th June, did nothing to ease the anxieties of the local people.

Hitler's forces had smashed across Europe and were now eagerly pushing at the frontiers of northern France. Squadrons of German aircraft had moved into airfields along the Channel coast. Cherbourg was just seventy miles across the Channel from the tip of Portland Bill. The newest and fastest of the Luftwaffe's bombers — the Junkers 88A, carrying three machine guns and 1,800 kg of bombs — could make the journey in fifteen minutes. The threat of invasion from the air was all too real.

THREE

Under Attack

In June 1940 Britain stood alone. The war was less than one year old and already Hitler had dominated most of Europe. German craft, troops and planes were being assembled to cross the Channel and invade Britain. First the Luftwaffe had to gain control of the skies, and the summer months of 1940 saw intense aerial fighting over southern Britain as attacks on Channel shipping increased and bombing raids began on coastal towns. It was to become known as The Battle of Britain.

With the news that Italy had entered the war on the side of Germany came the area's first Red Warning, when in the early hours of the 10th June anti-aircraft fire from ships in the Channel sent local defence units into action. Although an attack did not materialise, it was to be their first taste of the real thing.

"HAVE AN AIR RAID SHELTER BUILT NOW!" ran the headline in the *Southern Times* of the 21st June 1940, warning that the first bombs had already fallen on the south coast, probably a reference to six enemy aircraft which had been sighted over Weymouth and Portland the day before and dropped six bombs harmlessly in the sea. The paper also published a list, "to cut out and keep somewhere safe", of centres where information about air raid casualties would be available .

The area's first bombs fell on the evening of Sunday, the 30th June, when Portlanders strolling in the evening sunshine heard the ominous drone of engines above as bombs began to fall. One came down at Chesil Cove and failed to explode, enforcing the closure of the Cliff School at Clovens Road until it could be de-activated. The rest fell in the sea.

But the following Thursday – the 4th July – the Luftwaffe was to make its presence felt with a vengeance. At 8.30 a.m Poppy Collins-Dryer left her home in Albert Terrace, Portland, to go to school. A few minutes later her mother Emily went shopping in Fortuneswell. As she started to climb the hill she could look down at Portland Harbour and the dockyard where her husband Bob was employed in the excavation of hillside tunnels. A recent addition to the Harbour during the past month had been a converted merchant ship – now a Royal Naval anti-aircraft gunship, the 5500 ton HMS *Foylebank* – which had been brought in to boost the area's coastal defences. At 8.40 a.m a formation of twenty Junkers 87 "Stuka" bombers roared out of the sun. Breaking formation, they dived at the *Foylebank* at anchor on Admiral's Buoy, unleashing the full force of their weaponry. Poppy was pulled into a neighbour's house to shelter, while Emily in hurrying home dropped her door key and could only watch in horror from her doorway as the guns and bombs ripped across the vessel.

Barely had the *Foylebank* opened fire in defence, than the Stukas made numerous direct hits, exploding her gun turrets and severing the power system. Twenty-three year old Leading Seaman Jack Mantle, his left leg shattered, continued to fire at the attacking aircraft with a hand gun. Three enemy planes were shot down before they veered away, leaving the *Foylebank* ablaze. Jack Mantle, mortally wounded, collapsed at his gun and died shortly afterwards. It was still only 8.48 a.m.

Cruelly, as dockyard workers emerged from their hillside shelter at the sound of the "all clear", one of the Stukas returned and its pilot released his last bomb over Castletown. More than 160 crew had been killed in the attack, and 10 civilians, including Bob Collins-Dryer.

The thick black smoke billowing across Portland Harbour from the stricken *Foylebank* as it sank lower into the water was visible for miles along the coast. Poppy, continuing on her way to school, shivered as it obliterated the sun.

The funerals of the civilians, all Portlanders, took place the following week. Because of the fear of further attacks only close family were requested to attend. Jack Mantle and his shipmates are also buried on the Island, in the Naval Cemetery below

Above: Part of a painting by John Hamilton showing Stukas dive-bombing HMS *Foylebank* in Portland Harbour in July 1940.

Below: The distinctive headstone of Acting Leading Seaman Jack Foreman Mantle, VC, in Portland Naval Cemetery.

the Verne. He was to be posthumously awarded the Victoria Cross, for his heroism on that summer morning.

On the very afternoon of the *Foylebank* raid German planes twice attacked a large convoy of British merchant ships bound from the Thames Estuary for Cardiff. More than fifty casualties were taken off these vessels as they limped into Weymouth Bay. The convoy re-formed and continued its voyage, only to be attacked again off Portland at midnight, this time by German E-Boats. Five ships were sunk in these three incidents, causing the Admiralty to ban further westbound convoys in the Channel.

One of the victims of the action, the SS *Hartlepool* struggled towards Weymouth but sank about 1,000 yards off the stone pier on the south side of the Harbour. Her superstructure, a conspicuous target, was bombed by enemy planes a month later and then removed, but the vessel itself, although marked by a buoy, proved an inconvenience for the rest of the war to other vessels making for Weymouth Harbour.

The lack of RAF support during the *Foylebank* attack made it clear that without the protection of a fighter squadron close to hand the Naval base at Portland would continue to be extremely vulnerable. Ironically, the grass airfield and gunnery training school at Warmwell was declared operational on the day of the attack, and the Spitfires of 609 Squadron took up occupation just two days later, augmented within a week by 152 Squadron. Impending attacks on coastal defences could now be deflected more quickly.

Closer to Weymouth and Portland, an airfield had been set up at Chickerell in the 1930's in conjunction with an Air Ministry bombing range off nearby Chesil Beach for the re-fuelling and re-arming of aircraft. Never used by fighter squadrons, the 2,400 ft grass strip was capable of landing aircraft up to the size of a Blenheim and was operational throughout the war years. Four Westland Lysander aircraft were based there for most of that time to provide reconnaissance for enemy shipping. Due to the Lysander's short take off and landing distance, its two-passenger capacity and fixed ladder, many people living locally believed the aircraft were used for landing Special Operations Executives (SOEs) in France, although nothing of this nature was ever confirmed. The area was built on in the 1950s.

Throughout July the Warmwell Spitfires intercepted enemy bombers engaged in attacking shipping off Portland. The noise of gunfire from aircraft in combat and the sight of undercarriages skimming chimney pots became not unfamiliar to the residents.

On the 24th July Weymouth was once again coping with large numbers of wounded as the result of an E-Boat attack, although the torpedoed SS *Meknes* was no ordinary merchant ship. The French liner had left Southampton five hours earlier with 102 crew and 1,200 French Navy personnel who had elected to return to their own, now occupied, country rather than joining the Free French forces in England. Clearly marked and brightly illuminated to avoid any mistake as to her nationality, the *Meknes* expected a safe passage to France. Off Portland that evening the liner was intercepted and fired on by a German E-Boat. The *Meknes* came to a standstill, signalled her name and nationality and awaited an explanation. None came : her attacker fired torpedoes and the French ship sank in minutes. Almost 900 survivors reached Weymouth and the casualty services coped once again with wounds and welfare, many of the Frenchmen being injured and some requiring admission to the Emergency Hospital at Portwey.

Dry land was not necessarily any safer. Areas of Admiralty property had been mined to thwart enemy invaders. A Portlander has a vivid memory of a RN Petty Officer who had gone AWOL from HMS *Osprey* only to fall victim to a mine as he reached the Red Gates at the Grove :

"On hearing a loud explosion I ran to see. The torso had been blown clear over the wall and lay blackened in the road, and pieces of burned flesh stuck to the stone wall of the Borstal. I was quickly moved on by Borstal Officers and Coastguards".

Three days later, Weymouth experienced its first air raid which, although carried out by a single aircraft, damaged 17 houses. Shortly after midnight on the 27th July six high explosive bombs were dropped, mainly in the Wyke Road area, one scoring a direct hit and completely demolishing No 12 Russell Avenue. The occupants, 18-year old Alan Quartermaine and his mother, had been in their

12 Russell Avenue, Weymouth, hours after the air raid of July 27th 1940.

Devastation at Westham Cross Roads, Weymouth, on August 11th 1940. Members of the rescue services are indicating the spot where a mother and her young baby were safely pulled from the wreckage – the child's faint cries had alerted the rescue squad.

kitchen when they heard whistling noises before the house. collapsed around them. Alan Quartermaine told the rescue service:

"I don't remember anything more until I came to with the top of the gas stove resting on my neck, and a wash basin from the bathroom on top of me . . . the electric light bulb was still burning close to my head."

He was able to crawl out of the wreckage unscathed, and his mother, rescued soon afterwards, was only slightly injured.

Battles in the Sky

August brought almost daily air battles. Early in the month the enemy concentrated its attacks on Channel shipping and on the 8th a coaling convoy proved to be – in the words of a Spitfire pilot sent to defend it – "too large a prize for the Hun to miss". He was shortly afterwards participating in a furious overhead air fight, but six ships were sunk and many damaged in massive dive-bombing attacks. These losses resulted in the Admiralty restricting all daylight movement of vessels in the English Channel.

It soon became apparent that enemy air presence

The junction of Newstead and Melbury Roads following the raid of August 11th 1940. Three houses were completely demolished and five others severely damaged. There was one fatality. Rescue and demolition squads spent many laborious hours clearing up the debris after the raid.

over the area formed a pattern, as the most serious raids seemed to take place on a Thursday or a Sunday. Thus it was on a bright sunny Sunday that the Luftwaffe next attacked. At 9.45 am on the 11th August, the Isle of Wight radar picked up a formation of more than 150 fighters and bombers on a flight path to Portland. The Luftwaffe had deployed two formations to Dover to divert RAF Squadrons from the main strike target of Portland, and seven Squadrons were hurriedly scrambled to intercept the convoy. The siren sounded at 10.21 a.m at the same time as RAF Spitfires and Hurricanes had engaged the Messerchmitts in combat, a diversion which allowed the Stukas to break formation and launch into a multi-directional and precise bombing operation.

The first bombs fell at 10.28 am. Private Doug Acutt recalled later :

"All Weymouth people learned what it was that day to feel the ground tremble beneath their feet and their houses quake and shudder".

Of the 57 bombs which fell, all were in the Chapelhay, Hope Square, Rodwell and Westham districts. 463 houses were damaged, 40 of which were completely destroyed. The Brewery of J A Devenish was rent in two. The fates must have been on the side of the residents of Rodwell — 19 bombs fell on the area, all of which failed to explode and were later proclaimed "duds"! Even more staggering was

Devenish's Brewery, Hope Square, after the raid of August 11th 1940. The adjacent John Groves Brewery was also damaged, although less seriously, and the company assisted its old rival and neighbour until repairs were effected.

that, despite the most incredible damage done to buildings and property, the raid caused only one fatal injury.

The rescue and casualty services came into their own, and many were to find reserves of strength and purpose to surprise even themselves. Ambulance Officer Wally Dennis won numerous commendations for leading a first aid party to the rescue of others whilst himself injured.

Portland fared no better – the Luftwaffe's target being the naval base – and 32 bombs fell in the dockyard area. The signal box on the Weymouth to Portland railway was hit, killing the signalman and damaging the track. Fires burned fiercely from a leakage where one of the Navy's 26 oil tanks had been punctured by flying shrapnel and the main pipe

line fractured. It was almost three hours before the fire was brought under control. One of the phenomena of the wartime raids was that this was the only occasion on which this major fuel installation – prominently clustered along the railway track to the docks – was damaged. The tanks were later clad in stonework. Years later a Portland man found himself in conversation with a German, who smiled when he learned he was talking to a Portlander. The German had been a Stuka pilot and asked :

"Are the oil tanks still there? If you only knew how hard we tried to hit those damn things – we used to run a competition!"

The backlash was felt in Chiswell and Fortuneswell – as well as being showered by droplets of black oil from the thick choking smoke, several houses, including St John's Vicarage, were damaged or completely demolished and the plate glass windows of shops shattered.

During the attack a Junkers 88 was hit by anti-aircraft fire as it bombed the Bill and — its crew having baled out — the plane came down at Blacknor. Locals remember rushing to the scene to find soldiers already surrounding it and preparing to cover the swastika markings. Spectators were sent away as it was feared that the enemy would return to ensure the aircraft's destruction, it being the Luftwaffe's very latest bomber.

"We went to the edge of the cliff and could see an airman swimming to shore under West Cliff, where soldiers from Blacknor were waiting for him on the rocks, but he never made it. He went under only about 100 yards from the shore".

One Underhill girl, out for a Sunday walk when the raid began, was invited into a neighbouring house where they huddled on the stairs, and "we sat, absolutely petrified, with the bombs screaming down and the guns firing all around". Returning to her own street after the "all clear", she recalls:

"What a shock I had. One of the houses was razed to the ground and another sliced in half. It was a miracle no-one was killed. My mother was beside herself with worry and after that I was only allowed to play just outside the door".

The mournful wail of the sirens, the drone of aircraft engines, the thud of ack-ack guns, the banshee shrieking of falling bombs, the juddering of the earth, the clatter of flying shrapnel. These sounds would become only too familiar.

Two days later, on the 13th August, 609 Squadron was in action again and claimed 13 "kills" on a day when some 300 Luftwaffe planes intent on attacking targets in southern England were routed. Important visitors to Dorset were to witness the demise of one of the enemy aircraft. Winston Churchill was inspecting the coastal defences between Exmouth and Weymouth in the belief that a German invasion was imminent. He was accompanied by Lieutenant General Alan Brooke, General Claude Auchinleck and Major General Bernard Montgomery. Brooke later wrote in his diary :

"We found a German plane which had just come down. Pilot was all burned up, but, as 500lb bomb was in the debris which was burning we did not stop long . . ."

Downed aircraft, both German and British, were a not uncommon sight around Weymouth and

Downed enemy aircraft. A Junkers JU88 bomber at Portland and a Dornier shot down at Fleet. Royal Engineers stand guard.

Portland. Although their crews were frequently killed or wounded, the planes fortunately seemed to fall on fields or open ground without further loss of life. One Messerschmitt 110 hit the cliffs at Portland with such an impact that both the machine and its pilot were completely buried.

The trained eyes of the Observer Corps watched the skies above Dorset throughout the war, their task being to recognise and plot all aircraft in the area. At Portland an Observers' Post was set up at New Ground, and later moved out to Portland Bill. The Corps was to be commended several times in the following years for assisting Allied planes home.

On the 15th August the sounds of the biggest battle yet over Dorset brought Weymouth and Portland people out of their homes regardless of the danger as the RAF sent some 40 enemy planes spinning into the Channel. British radar was extremely effective in detecting approaching enemy aircraft, and the German bombers attempted to stop the RAFs swift response by bombing airfields near the coast. It was Warmwell's turn to be hit on the 25th, but a warning had been received from intelligence sources and the damage was not serious. Warmwell pilots were always at something of a disadvantage being so close to the coast, as they had little time to gain height before meeting the enemy.

Pilots were of considerably more value than the aircraft they flew, and it was not unusual to see an airman descending by parachute being circled by an RAF plane until he had been safely picked up from the Channel. The life expectancy of these courageous young men who flew Spitfires and Hurricanes was short. They were later immortalised as "The Few" and more than twenty lie in carefully tended graves in a quiet corner of Warmwell Churchyard. Of the airfield they flew from there is little trace. Gravel extraction sites and housing have since taken over the wartime action station and only a few derelict buildings still stand as a reminder of Warmwell's role in the Battle of Britain.

By mid-September the Battle was turning in favour of the RAF and Hitler was forced to postpone his invasion plan, codenamed "Operation Sealion". The Germans began to concentrate on the heavy bombing of British cities, which in the winter and spring of 1940-41 became known as "The Blitz". But locally the raids continued, and in the Westham area oil bombs were used for the first time, causing fierce and instantaneous fires.

Ever adaptable, local families soon became used to getting on with their lives, despite the constant threat of the familiar dreaded drone of approaching enemy aircraft.

Bombs had often started to fall before the warning siren sounded and, so as not to get caught out, many would spend every night in their Anderson shelter, sleeping as best they could in an upright position on wooden benches. One Fortuneswell family, whose home overlooked Chesil and the Mere, found an early warning system in their elderly grandmother who would sit all day in the window from where she could see the anti-aircraft gun emplacements. On receiving a warning of raiders approaching the gunners would hurry to their posts. Her cry of "The soldiers are running!" had not only her own household but the whole street safely into their shelters well before the siren sounded!

Although many houses were damaged during the summer of 1940 there were miraculously no serious casualties. One Sunday a surprise attack by 25 Heinkel HE111's reduced the unoccupied St John's School at Fortuneswell to rubble, severely disrupting the schooling of Underhill children for the next five years.

Education became a very haphazard affair, attendance often being part-time. Where schools had been damaged or destroyed, classrooms had to be shared, and not only could the school buildings not accommodate all the pupils at once but neither could the air raid shelters. The dug-out trenches were cramped and unpleasant – the only good thing was the barley sugar sweet given to each child if the air raid warning lasted more than an hour or confinement to the shelter coincided with a mealtime!

September brought the first incendiary bombs to Weymouth, small powerful devices dropped in clusters. They could lie undetected until the delayed action explosive they contained caused them to burst into flames. They created havoc when dropped in built-up areas, and fires after raids became such a problem that a Fire Guard scheme was introduced early in 1941 making it compulsory to have someone on duty in buildings and streets ready to extinguish fires or summon help if they got beyond control.

As The Blitz continued Weymouth and Portland became the target of indiscriminate "tip and run" raids at any hour of the night or day. This type of raid was carried out by a single aircraft on an uneventful mission of minelaying or reconnaissance, carrying one or two bombs along to relieve the tedium for the pilot. Shortly after noon on the 21st October a lone raider unloaded two high explosive bombs over the town. The Southern National Garage in Edward Street sustained irreparable structural damage and thirty neighbouring homes were destroyed. Three men and two children died in the bombing.

The voice of the Prime Minister, Winston Chur-

A single enemy plane dropped one oil and three high explosive bombs in the Edward Street area of Weymouth at the end of October 1940. The Southern National Bus Garage and eight houses were demolished, five people died. Over a hundred houses were damaged, of which nineteen had to be pulled down.

chill, gave comfort and inspiration during those fearful days. A Weymouth man – aged 6 in 1940 – remembers sitting quietly rigid whenever those commanding tones came crackling over the wireless. "No-one had to tell me to be quiet. I just knew."

Chapelhay's Worst Raid

It was to hear Churchill speak at 9 pm on a Sunday evening that families in the Chapelhay area gathered round their wireless sets. Chapelhay was to have more than its fair share of damage and tragedy during the war years, and an attack by a single aircraft on that November night was the first to really wreak havoc in the tightly packed district.

Two parachute mines – the first to be used in Weymouth or Portland – descended without noise, but on contact created a blast which could be felt half a mile away and shattered windows on the seafront. Whereas bombs dropped in earlier raids had destroyed one or two houses, parachute mines were capable of razing whole streets. Of the twelve killed, all but one were residents of Franchise Street. 879 houses suffered damage, 77 of which were totally destroyed. Holy Trinity Schools were hit and the children were temporarily housed in the old Technical School in Commercial Road (now the Arts Centre).

In terms of damage to property, this was the severest raid Weymouth suffered in the whole of the war. But there were also many injuries, and local

Above and Below: The effects of the land mine dropped on Chapelhay, November 17th 1940.

Rescue Parties, helped by volunteers from Portland, Dorchester and Bridport, worked throughout that night and for the next two days until all those missing had been found. St Thomas Street was littered with broken glass along its entire length and rescue parties made their way to Chapelhay along Westwey Road, fearing that the Town Bridge had been hit. A film was showing to a packed house at the Regent Theatre when pieces of plaster came down from the ceiling. Such was people's acceptance of bombing raids by now that those who stood up in alarm were told by others in the audience to sit down and stop spoiling the film.

Amazingly, despite the scattered bombs which affected most parts of the town at one time or another, none of Weymouth and Portland's vital bridges were to suffer serious damage. It is highly likely that Weymouth Harbour was the target of the November raid, as bombs which were dropped on Rodwell a couple of days later (without serious effect) were described in a German propaganda leaflet as "an attack on Harbour Installations at Weymouth". The fact of Weymouth and Portland being three parts surrounded by the Channel proved

SOUTHERN TIMES, FRIDAY, NOVEMBER 22, 1940.

WEYMOUTH EDITION

BLACK-OUT TIMES

Today (Friday)—5·41 p.m. to 8.6 a.m.

Saturday—5·40 p.m. to 8·8 a.m.

Sunday—5·39 p.m. to 8·10 a.m.

Monday—5·38 p.m. to 8·11 a.m.

Tuesday—5·37 p.m. to 8·13 a.m.

Wednesday—5·36 p.m. to 8·14 a.m.

Thursday—5·35 p.m. to 8.16 a.m.

Southern Times

Vol. LXXXVIII., No. 4727 (Est. 1852)　　FRIDAY, NOVEMBER 22, 1940　　Registered by the G.P.O. as a Newspaper.　Price 2d.

LONE NIGHT RAIDER WRECKS STREET, CHURCHES, SCHOOL

RESCUE SQUADS WORK THROUGH NIGHT

RESIDENTS of a South of England town, sitting snug and warm in their homes at night, had their thoughts and conversations shattered by the roar of an enemy bomber, possibly Italian, flying low. A large high explosive was dropped, gutting houses, damaging two churches and a school, blowing out many shop windows, and killing and injuring a number of people.

The explosive fell in a back-garden rectangle formed by four streets of houses. Rescue squads were called, and worked all through the night. Helmets saved many from injury, as large pieces of debris crashed whenever anti-aircraft guns fired.

By morning rescue work was well in ... but there were still some buried ...

Joan Boniface's mother died some years ago. Her father and two younger sisters are living at Littlehampton. She ...

shop to bring out a mattress and some soiled clothing.

The Right Spirit

A butcher's company had the front and back blown out of their shop, one wall down, and all the top floor off. But they are going to carry on.

Seeing the bold "Business as usual" notices outside, I climbed into the shop, asked Mr. "Mac," the manager: "How's business?" Was surprised when he answered. "Just as good as any other Tuesday." He was cheerful about working on in his now very light and airy premises. "As long as we've got a block, the scales, and a till we're all right," he beamed.

I spoke to the Vicar of the church which has been severely damaged. He is going to carry on services in the hall of another building, does not know when his own church will be ready again. "It all depends on the diocesan architect's report," he remarked.

SPITFIRE FUND

Spitfire Fund to date totals £2,987 16s 0d. Area figures and latest donations are given belc.

Dorchester & district £1,561 8 10

Weymouth & district ...£770 10 2

Swanage & district £655 17 0

Per "Southern Times":

Weymouth Post Officer and Engineering staffs (12th donation) 2 2 0

Mr. Bert Haysham 1 0 0

R. Mutch, C. Bye, S. Mutch, and R. Coals 4

Per Mr. R. Gray, Portland: Mrs. Dowell, 1/-; Mrs. L. Knight, 1/-; Mrs. Blunders, 2 6 .... 4 6

Money collected by Cadet ...

Part of the front page of the local weekly *Southern Times* reporting the Chapelhay raid. It was described as having taken place in a 'South of England town', but the names and addresses were easily identified by those living locally.

to be its saviour. "Without doubt the sea saved us," says Mary Shipman. "If all the bombs that went into the sea had exploded on land there would have been nothing left".

The vital anti-submarine work at HMS *Osprey* was under threat from these constant attacks and it was decided in January to move the establishment to the less exposed location of Dunoon in Scotland.

The whole of the town area from Wyke to Radipole was affected on the 16th and 17th January when bombers scattered some 3,000 incendiary bombs, causing damage to 274 buildings and major fires at V H Bennett and the A1 Stores. Nine people were injured.

During the first months of 1941 local people were to witness clouds of bombers passing almost nightly over the coast. Their mission was to cause devastation and chaos in Bristol and the cities of the west Midlands, and their regular drone became known as "The Bristol Express".

Easter brought a burst of savage raids and the first of these, on Easter Monday brought tragedy to the Island. Bombers dropped high explosive bombs over the Underhill and Grove areas, causing considerable damage to the Borstal Institution, and destroying the Kingsway Hotel in Queens Road — in use as accommodation for servicemen — together with many homes in the closely inhabited area. Poppy Collins-Dryer lived in nearby Albert Terrace, and recalls :

"All our windows were blown in and the beds covered with glass and debris. An aunt lived the

35

Anti-invasion measures being strengthened early in 1941 with the installation of a 9.2 inch gun at Portland's East Weares Battery.

A German photograph showing bombs falling on Portland Harbour (Chequers Fort is visible on the left), first published in a German air raid wardens' magazine called *Die Sirene*.

other side of the Hotel and part of her roof was blown away. There were severed limbs and torsos all over her rooms".

Rescuers, aided by parties from Weymouth, worked until the next morning to recover all the bodies.

The following night it was Weymouth's turn to be battered by the raiders. High explosive and incendiary bombs were unloaded in the Rodwell, Westham and Radipole districts, causing considerable damage to many homes, from which there were some incredible escapes. Sadly, those killed were the ticket collector on duty at Rodwell Station and four soldiers asleep in Radipole House at Fernhill Avenue, which received a direct hit, although more than 100 soldiers who had been billeted there had moved on a few days earlier. As rescue squads searched the ruins of the station for the missing railwaymen, enemy planes were overhead and a bomb was heard to fall. There was no explosion

and work continued. Some time later a nearby householder reported that his ceilings were all down for no apparent reason, and closer inspection by the rescue squad revealed that the bomb they heard falling had gone clean through the house and into the ground beneath. Fortunately for all concerned, it failed to explode. Safe in his Anderson shelter, the owner had not even felt its impact. A number of similar incidents were caused by unexploded bombs.

Bombs were not the only form of attack used by the Luftwaffe upon the long suffering locals – civilians going about their everyday business would often be machine gunned in the street by attacking aircraft. Terrifying this must undoubtedly have been, but it induced some surprising reactions. A Weymouth lady remembers that when caught in machine gun fire which ripped across St Thomas Street, she was more outraged than afraid: "There I was, lying face down in the street, and I just felt so cross that they had disrupted my day like that!"

Clearing up and getting back to normal at Whitehead's Torpedo Factory following the raid of May 1st 1941. Despite the apparent destruction, little vital machinery was damaged and no one was injured.

Young boys at the Grove, after watching German planes shooting at the Borstal and C Quarters, would rush to recover the bullets and prise them out of the stone walls, still too hot to hold!

Such attacks, though, often caused injury or death, and a lunchtime bombing raid on Whitehead's Torpedo Factory on 1st May, while resulting in no casualties as the buildings were empty, was followed by a single aircraft returning and machine gunning pedestrians in the Portland Road area near Ferry Bridge. Two men were killed. Although the factory was severely damaged in the raid, no vital plant was lost, but it did speed plans to disperse some of the torpedo production to other locations.

Early May brought almost daily bombings. An evening raid on the 3rd caused fierce fires in the town area, the *Southern Times* office, Hawkes Freeman Furniture Stores, and Webb Major's Timber Yard being severely damaged. A high explosive bomb in Ashton Road destroyed houses and killed two residents, and four direct hits on the Portland Railway put the track out of action for a day.

Heavy raids over the following days left residents shaken and fearful – the destruction of Weymouth and Portland seemed to be the Luftwaffe's sole objective!

Then – as if the Chapelhay area had not suffered enough – the densely populated community was to have two devastating raids within as many days. In the early hours of the 9th May, after the "all clear" had sounded, a lone aircraft filtered radar cover and dropped five bombs, two falling in Oakley Place demolishing three houses, and three exploding the trench shelters of Holy Trinity School. Mrs Lilian Adnam and her five daughters had returned home from their shelter at the end of the warning and were killed when their house was hit. A four year old boy was the seventh fatality. The bombing damaged 152 houses.

The Luftwaffe struck again just two days later

A pair of unique photographs taken from almost the same spot in Ashton Road, off Chickerell Road, Weymouth. The top one was taken before the war, its companion shortly after an air raid on May 3rd 1941 completely demolished the terraced houses on the right hand side.

Relaxing at the Greenhill end of the beach despite the omnipresent shore defences.

when shortly after midnight on the 12th May, 32 high explosive bombs and hundreds of incendiaries were scattered across Wyke and Rodwell. Six homes were completely destroyed and nearly 100 damaged. Water and gas mains were fractured. Rescue and First Aid parties scoured the rubble through the night and into the next afternoon until the bodies of the six killed were recovered.

The early hours of the 15th May brought the largest bomb of the war to Weymouth. The one and three-quarter ton heavy calibre high explosive bomb was dropped by a lone aircraft just after 3 a.m. at the foot of Boot Hill near the Sidney Hall. Penetrating deeply into the soft ground, the effect of its mighty explosion was cushioned, and little damage was caused to properties other than the Sidney Hall itself.

Tip and run raids continued sporadically throughout the summer of 1941, Chapelhay was again the victim of high explosive bombs. On Sunday 13th July a 10-year old boy was killed in the raid, and another 434 houses damaged, 51 beyond repair.

Despite such devastation, morale and determination remained high in the local population. After a raid, even among those who had been bombed-out, the attitude tended to be one of "You won't get *me*, Hitler!". When the staff of the Franchise Street Co-op store arrived one morning to find the shop windows blown in and groceries strewn everywhere, they were back in business within the hour. A pub landlord whose windows suffered the same fate simply swept up the glass and carried on business with his bars open to the street. It was summer, and although the bombs fell, the holidaymakers were absent and much of the seafront was out of bounds, Weymouth's inhabitants were determined to enjoy some of its facilities and the military authorities were persuaded to set aside an area of the beach for bathing each day between 2 and 7 pm.

The Weymouth Borough Medical Officer, Dr Gordon Wallace, and the Sanitary Inspector, Mr Fanner,

Above: Chapelhay, Weymouth, scene of so much air raid damage, was hit again on May 9th 1941. The photograph shows Oakley Place after the attack.

Below: The Royal Adelaide Hotel, Abbotsbury Road, Westham, home of Weymouth's mayor, John Goddard, was partly demolished by bombs in November 1941.

thought it timely to issue a leaflet to residents listing preparations they should make in case the public water supply and sewers were ruptured by bombing. Buckets should be used in place of lavatories, the contents to be buried daily in the garden or allotment or emptied in the public gardens or the Harbour!

Weymouth's Mayor, John Goddard, gained first hand experience of the discomfort and suffering of the townspeople when, on the night of the 1st November, four high explosive bombs caused chaos in Westham, tearing apart his home, the Adelaide Hotel. Trapped by debris in his bedroom, it was nearly an hour before the rescue party, headed by one of his own macebearers, was able to cut him free. In a recorded broadcast to the people of Weymouth, Massachusetts, Councillor Goddard recounted his experience that night : "I heard one of them (the rescue party) say "Is he all right?" and the other chap said "He's swearing a bit so he must be all right"' (the Medical Officer had given the Mayor a shot of morphine when he heard the language!). He and his wife were treated for shock and minor injuries at Weymouth & District Hospital. The raid caused three deaths and a further 171 houses were damaged.

In a letter a few days later, the Mayor – his injured right hand impairing his signature – said "I now have my own experience of the effects of bombing and the work of our Civil Defence Services . . . it gives me the greatest confidence for the future".

His confidence was to be echoed by the whole country on a much wider scale within a few weeks.

FOUR

Steps to a Victory

A surprise attack by the Japanese Air Force on the U.S. Naval Base at Pearl Harbour in the Pacific in the first week of December 1941 forced America to declare war on Japan. On the 11th December Japan's allies, Germany and Italy, declared war on the United States.

The entry of America on the side of Great Britain was to give a renewed strength to the nation, weakened by relentless air raids and hardships.

By the beginning of 1942 every major power was involved in World War II, which had become a truly global conflict. But for Britain the immediate threat of invasion was over. Germany had failed to destroy the RAF and The Blitz had failed to destroy the morale of the British people. Eventual victory, which had looked distant and at times unattainable, seemed within touching distance. Hitler's forces were by now massively deployed in the Balkans, the Soviet Union and North Africa, and consequently Britain enjoyed a brief respite from the unrelenting bombing raids of 1940 and 1941.

On the surface life may have seemed peaceful, but unbeknown to those who lived in the area it was playing a vital role in foiling the enemy. The vacated buildings of HMS *Osprey* at Portland had been occupied by HMS *Attack*, operational base for Coastal Forces for over a year, and its fleet of Motor Gun Boats (MGB's) had been busy intercepting E-Boats in the Channel and safely escorting shipping through the vulnerable bottleneck between the Bill and the Cherbourg Peninsula. Minesweepers moving in and out of Portland Harbour to clear mines in Lyme Bay were a daily sight. By January 1942, HMS *Attack* could boast an anti-invasion fleet of motor gun boats, launches, and anti-submarine and minesweeping trawlers.

It had been part of Churchill's policy since Dunkirk to preoccupy the Germans by short, sharp, scattered raids, and small raiding parties in Motor Torpedo Boats would regularly slip out of Weymouth under cover of darkness bound for enemy occupied territory across the Channel. The stealthy MTB's could cut engines ten miles out and glide silently in to shore, allowing highly trained commandos to carry out their top secret missions. Most of the locals were unaware of the comings and goings of these craft, but would often see the men of the raiding parties ashore in their unconventional uniforms.

Bruneval Raid

For some time German ships had been encountered in the Channel having gone undetected by British coastal radar. Intelligence revealed that the enemy had been using an apparatus known as a Wurzburg to jam radar so successfully that by February 1942 our own coastal radar was all but ineffective. Counter measures were a matter of urgency and aerial photographs identified a Wurzburg sited on an accessible cliff top at Bruneval on the Channel coast of northern France. Plans were made to capture the apparatus for examination. Full scale rehearsals for "Operation Biting" were held at Redcliff Point, Osmington. On the 27th February, 120 men of 'C' Company of the 2nd Battalion of the 1st Parachute Brigade were dropped by parachute from twelve Whitley bombers. Accompanying them was an RAF Radar Mechanic, whose expertise would enable them to identify the Wurzburg's key components.

Under gunfire, Flt. Sgt. Cox attempted to dismantle the Wurzburg, but with only ten minutes to carry out the operation, some sections had to be removed by force. It was carried through several inches of snow to the beach, where, still under fire, naval craft evacuated the paratroopers and their cargo. Two members of 'C' Company were killed in the raid. Of the two German prisoners taken, one was a Wurzburg operator who assisted in the piecing together of the apparatus back at the Air Ministry. Further examination of it was carried out at the

top secret Telecommunications Research Establishment at Worth Matravers in Dorset which revealed valuable information about the state of the enemy's radar technology. Four months later the Research Establishment was transferred inland to Malvern for fear that the Germans might plan a similar raid in retaliation.

Renewed enemy air attacks were heralded at the end of March. On the 23rd two bombs were dropped harmlessly in the sea off Castle Cove, but the raiders found their target at Portland. Thirteen high explosive bombs caused widespread damage to naval property and buildings in the Underhill area. The Methodist School, recently repaired and reopened following previous raids, was hit again.

The Home Guard was credited with bringing down one of the bombers as it turned low over Ferry Bridge, where men from Whiteheads were manning one of four twin mounted Brownings.

"All four guns opened up on the raider at a rate of 1,100 rounds per gun per minute. Burning, it turned back towards Portland where all anti-aircraft guns within range opened fire". John Butcher was in the Regal Cinema at Fortuneswell when the sound of the guns brought the audience into the street.

"The plane was on fire and seemed to be circling for a place to come down away from the houses. It crashed, blazing, into W F Davies' Builder's Yard at Brandy Row. The pilot baled out but he was too low for his parachute to open."

Commandos training at Osmington for 'Operation Biting', the successful raid on a German radar post at Bruneval in 1942. Commandos were billeted with local families and one unit, No 4 (Army) Commando, was actually founded at Weymouth in July 1940, with its HQ at the Pavilion Theatre, where there is now a commemorative plaque in the foyer.

Mobile canteens and the new British Restaurants provided hot meals for those who had lost everything they possessed in air raids.

Film was scarce in wartime and few photographs exist of air raid damage on Portland. This view shows some of the havoc caused by the 'Black Easter' raids of April 1941 when the Borstal was hit and much other property destroyed by high explosive bombs.

When police and air raid wardens arrived on the scene they found an elderly member of the Home Guard standing over the wreckage with a fixed bayonet, ready to bar the way to anyone attempting to leave the plane. Three Germans were dead inside it. A woman who looked out of her window some distance away saw the body of the dead pilot sprawled in her garden.

St Nazaire

At the end of March a 41-year-old Portland man was to take part in a courageous and successful raid on a strategic German naval base on the Atlantic coast of France – and be one of the few to live to tell the tale!

Daniel Pike was a Petty Officer First Class on HMS *Campbeltown*, a destroyer which had been converted into a streamlined armour-plated, highly explosive weapon for the purpose of ramming the 35 feet thick steel gates of the Great Normandie Dock at St Nazaire, the only dock capable of taking

the most powerful battleship in the world, the German *Tirpitz*, for repairs. The *Campbeltown's* bows had been fitted with delayed action charges to explode the vessel after she had been evacuated. Backed up by motor launches, gunboats and bomber squadrons, and with all guns and cannons blazing, the *Campbeltown* approached St Nazaire under the concentrated fire of enemy defences. At 01.34 hours she crashed into the outer gate, allowing gunboats and commandos to wreak havoc on the inner dock and shore installations. When the *Campbeltown*, jammed into the gate, finally exploded, she took 400 Germans with her. But tragically almost as many British commandos and sailors were killed. Many were captured, and the raid was noted for its outstanding acts of bravery. Mountbatten said of the incident: "I know of no other case in naval or military annals of such effective damage being inflicted so swiftly with such economy of force." The Normandie Dock was never again used by the Germans.

Daniel Pike, who sustained slight injuries in the raid, was mentioned in Despatches and awarded the Croix de Guerre for his part. He completed the war with a brave and impressive record.

Dive Bombers

Maundy Thursday, the 2nd April 1942, brought Weymouth's first dive bombing attack. In terms of civilian loss of life this was the area's worst single raid of the entire war. Fifty five aircraft ripped apart the town area, devastating parts of Greenhill, Newstead Road, and Nicholas Street, the Fox Inn and the offices of the *Dorset Echo* being among those buildings reduced to rubble. Water and gas mains and electricity cables were damaged. Twenty were killed in the attack and sixty injured, but there is no doubt that the new indoor Morrison Shelter saved many lives that day. Families were found safe inside these steel "cages" although their homes had collapsed around and on top of them. Rescue parties were brought in from Dorchester, Bridport and Wareham to assist in recovering the dead and injured, and the 15th Welsh Regiment helped to clear the debris. Patients from the over-flowing Weymouth and District Hospital were the next day moved to hospitals in adjoining counties to make room for possible further casualties should there be another attack. Understandably, the *Echo*

Above: The remains of the Fox Inn, St Nicholas Street, demolished in a raid on April 2nd 1942, together with neighbouring houses and the *Dorset Daily Echo* works. Note the cupboard perilously perched on a collapsed linoleum-covered floor.

Below: Although this house in Glen Avenue, Weymouth, completely collapsed round its occupants on April 2nd 1942 they were rescued practically unscathed from the sturdy steel Morrison shelter visible in the centre of the room.

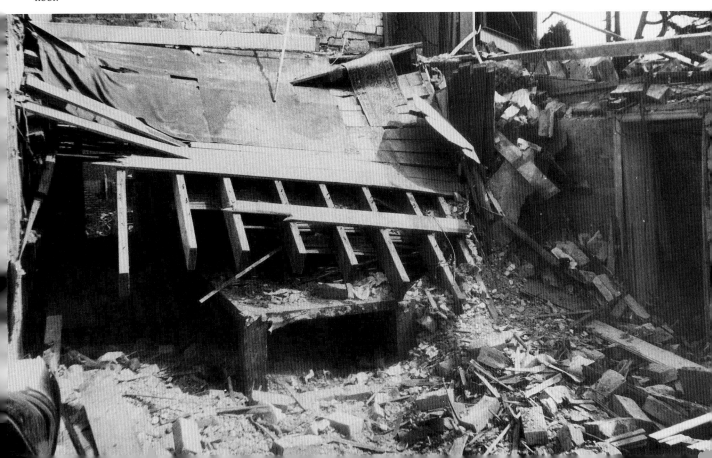

was not in circulation on that day, but the next day and for the rest of the war it was printed at the Bournemouth plant.

There were of course lulls, but they brought scant respite to the Civil Defence Casualty services. For them it was a chance to take part in training exercises, demonstrations, lectures, first-aid and anti-gas courses. At one of the two depots – "Nine Elms" at Westham – they even managed annual gardening shows. The Casualty Services' second depot was in a hut at the other end of town, an ex-Weymouth College property in Cranford Avenue.

Various of these College buildings saw war service, the public school having closed for good in 1940. De-gaussing work went on there in the early months and later the buildings became an emergency hospital. One of the College's most famous "old boys" was G H Stainforth, who in 1931 broke the world airspeed record as a member of the Schneider Trophy team. In 1942 the news came through that Wing Commander Stainforth had been shot down and killed in the Middle East.

In spite of the nightly blackouts, the shortages of just about everything, and never knowing when the next air raid might be, there was still enough enthusiasm to assist the war effort. Young and old participated in parades, fancy dress, concerts, dances and competitions – all aimed at raising money. In the 1942 "Warships Weeks" Weymouth set its sights on adopting the submarine HMS *Rorqual*, the "price" of which was £350,000. The town surpassed itself by exceeding this figure and the submarine duly became Weymouth's "own" warship. With a smaller population to collect donations from, Portland went all out for a vessel in a lower price range and the Island's prize was the trawler-minesweeper HMS *Kingston Onyx*. These almost carnival-like activities provided a little frivolity in a period of increasing drabness and austerity.

Ironically, soon after the tremendously successful Warships Weeks came news of the sinking of HMS *Dorsetshire* by dive bombers in the Indian Ocean and fundraising began all over again to replace the ship with another bearing the county's name.

In June enemy bombers returned. In the early hours of Sunday the 28th June it was the old village of Wyke Regis which was blasted. The centuries-old Ship Inn was blown apart and other houses in Shrubbery Lane extensively damaged. The wife of the landlord was among the five killed in the raid. Local man Dick Abbott recalls a strange thing about the incident:

"When the pub in Shrubbery Lane was bombed the village next morning was covered with feathers. An interesting phenomenon was that for some years afterwards woodworm in new furniture and timber was unusually prevalent in the Wyke area!".

Houses on the Southlands Estate were damaged the same night, and a woman died at Bradford Road. In all, 10 bombs fell, causing the demolition of 20 houses and damaging 50.

The following night hundreds of incendiary bombs were dropped in Westham. John Coleman's garden was his pride and joy, and his son Graham recalls his father's fury when incendiaries fell among his gooseberry bushes and set them alight just as a prize crop was ready for picking. But gardeners who did have a glut of fruit were encouraged to take the surplus to the Old Town Hall, where a government-sponsored Jam Making scheme saved it going to waste.

Setback at Dieppe

On the other side of the world, the summer of 1942 saw Allied forces victorious over Japan in the Pacific, but closer to home an attempted assault on the French coast by the Allies proved a tragic failure. This was the Dieppe Raid – codenamed "Operation Jubilee".

The ill-fated "Jubilee" was planned in April, and practice landings involving infantry landing ships from Portland were carried out at Bridport, Lulworth, Worbarrow, Osmington and Weymouth Bay throughout the summer until early August. Winston Churchill intended that it should be "A reconnaissance in force to test the enemy defences and to discover what resistance would be met to seize a port." It also provided an opportunity to test 30 of the new Churchill tanks, which he had inspected at Lulworth Camp that month.

Dieppe was chosen by Combined Operations HQ as an ideal target for a seaborne assault, being within range of British airfields from where fighter cover could be mounted. The aim was to get in and get out within a day, causing as much damage as possible to enemy defences.

The date was set for the 19th August. Minesweepers had cleared the route for the assault force of 252 ships – including support craft from Weymouth – carrying over 6000 men to make a 3 a.m landing. Sixty squadrons of fighter aircraft were on standby.

But the attempt to seize Dieppe was lost on its beaches, with men and tanks pinned down beneath the sea wall under relentless fire from German guns. Scattered groups of men and some six tanks gallantly managed to surmount the sea wall and inflict damage in the town, but these were unsupported by back-up forces. The bombardment on the other side of the Channel rattled doors and windows in Weymouth and Portland but the guns of the British destroyers and fighter aircraft did not even dent the formidable enemy defences. By 9 a.m. the decision to withdraw was made, but it was nearly two hours later that landing craft were able to move in and evacuate the survivors.

The operation was costly. Nearly 4000 men, over 3000 of them Canadians, were lost, with 106 allied aircraft shot down, and the British destroyer *Berkeley*, hit by cross fire, failing to return. The Germans lost only 600 men.

The raid floundered due to insufficient planning and intelligence. Information of the geography of the beachhead and the strength of German defences had been inadequate. Assault troops needed the fire power of tanks and armoured vehicles as back up. Out of the disaster, important lessons were learned which were to prove invaluable in the planning of

Landing craft manoeuvres in Portland Harbour, February 1942. These were the key craft of the D-Day invasion force, but only after the lessons learned from the disastrous Dieppe Raid in August 1942 were they successfully used.

the invasions of Sicily and Normandy. "Dieppe", said *The New York Times*, "was where brave men died without hope for the sake of proving that there is a wrong way to invade. They will have their share of glory when the right way is tried".

In the meantime the eyes of the world were on a small town in Egypt, 60 miles west of Alexandria. In July of 1942, the Eighth Army had established a position at El Alamein, preventing the advance of the German and Italian armies towards Cairo and the Nile delta. Having stubbornly refused to move until he had enough armoury to ensure an even chance of success, General Montgomery led a relentless assault on enemy positions in October. Rommel's attempts at a counter attack were foiled and after ten bitter days the Afrika Korps was defeated. The Eighth Army went from victory to victory and in May 1943 the German army in Tunisia surrendered, clearing the way for the invasion of Sicily. Churchill was to say of the battle: "Before Alamein we never had a victory. After Alamein we never had a defeat". The campaign was the turning point for the allied forces, boosting morale back in Britain where the news was received with elation. "Monty" was hailed as a hero, and Churchill asked that church bells be rung throughout the country to celebrate the victory!

But the people of Portland found themselves at the mercy of their own enemy in the December of 1942. All through the morning of the 13th – a Sunday – the sea had been boiling up above surging ground swells, and just after 11 a.m started to filter through the pebbles above the clay ridge. Within an hour waves of up to 60 feet gushed over the top of Chesil Bank, through the Cove House Inn, smashing away stone walls, carrying along boats, railway sleepers, fishermens' huts and hurling them hundreds of yards. The water was soon 5 feet deep in Victoria Square and Chiswell, where many were stranded in upstairs rooms, as more than a hundred houses were flooded. The Island was without gas and cut off from the mainland. It was the worst flood in living memory and was soon being compared with tales of the famous "Great Gale" of 1824.

During the afternoon the waters subsided, leaving mud, shingle and debris a foot deep. Geared up by wartime to react quickly in an emergency, Council workers, Civil Defence Rescue Parties, Borstal boys and soldiers worked together to get the road open

to traffic the same evening. The ladies of the WVS were soon on the scene distributing hot food, dry clothes and bedding. The Cove House Inn, despite its frontage being swept away and the sea having passed through its ground floor, was open for business at 7 p.m! The gas supply was re-connected within 36 hours, but it was three days before the rail link with the mainland could re-open.

The unique geography of Chesil Beach had advantages though, and the bombing range established there in the 1930s was the chosen setting for tests of a prototype dam-busting bomb designed to skim across the surface of water and explode on impact with a dam.

The boffin behind what would become known as "the Bouncing Bomb" was scientist Barnes Wallis of Vickers Armstrong's Aviation Division at Weybridge. In the first test on the 4th December, a low-flying Wellington bomber from Warmwell dropped two steel spheres across the flat water of the Fleet, but both broke up on contact with the surface. Two further test drops also failed, but on the 10th January 1943 a strengthened version of the bomb successfully skimmed the water. Over the next few weeks a wooden sphere was tested and by the end of February the team had succeeded in bouncing the "bomb" some 1300 yards across the Fleet. Steel versions were then used in a series of trial runs in which the bomb aimer could send the dummy skimming accurately across the surface, and by the time trials concluded on the 9th March it began to look as though the "bouncing bomb" had a future as a useful and effective weapon.

Testing was to be continued in Kent where the "bomb" would be subjected to more realistic conditions – a move much welcomed by the swanherd at Abbotsbury, where the Wellington's 300 mph approach flight had been disrupting breeding!

The Spring of 1943 brought the good news that the Bouncing Bomb had been used with spectacular success by Lancaster bombers in dam-busting raids in the Ruhr Valley, breaching the vital Mohne and Eder Dams.

By then, however, the south coast of England was under invasion – but it was to be an invasion of the friendliest kind. One and a quarter million American servicemen were to pass through Great Britain before 1945 and their arrival in Weymouth and Portland was to have a lasting impact.

FIVE

A Friendly Invasion

The first American troops arrived in Britain in January 1942, a month after the "Day of Infamy" at Pearl Harbour had brought the United States into the war. At first they were few in number and received a fairly indifferent welcome, due in part to the attitude of the war-weary British who felt they had been fighting alone and that the Americans should have entered the war earlier. In an era when few from either country had ever crossed the Atlantic there was also a misconception held by both sides that, because they shared a common language "they were the same as us".

Some attempt was made to prepare Britain for the coming "friendly invasion" of GIs. In the autumn of 1942 the army organised a series of public lectures aimed at "furthering the understanding between the

American soldiers and British sailors jointly training in landing craft in Weymouth Bay.

English and American peoples", but attendance was sparse at both Weymouth's Guildhall and the Jubilee Hall, Portland. The local people would have been astounded (and possibly more attentive) had they realised that less than a year later Dorset would be playing host to more than half a million American servicemen.

Secret planning of the Allied assault on Hitler's "Fortress Europe" had been under way since 1940 and intensive preparations for the execution of the invasion, to be known as D-Day, now began.

Late in 1943 General Dwight D. Eisenhower of the US Army was appointed Supreme Commander of the Allied Invasion Forces. "Operation Overlord", the codename for the invasion, was to be an amphibious assault on the beaches of Normandy. Originally a plan to capture three beachheads, it was expanded to five, spanning a 60-mile wide area. On the east side, British and Canadian troops were to land on three beaches codenamed Gold, Juno and Sword. Their training began in south-east England. The American forces were to take two separate areas on either side of the Vire River estuary in the west, codenamed Omaha and Utah. These were the men who would pour into south-west England to practise landings on the coast. "Overlord" was to be the largest amphibious invasion in history.

Its success depended on landing vast numbers of troops on the beaches swiftly, and protecting their advance by naval and aerial bombardment of the enemy's defences. The key vessels of the invasion fleet were landing craft, the purpose-built ships which came into their own during the Second World War. Months of training began for the men who would struggle ashore from them in full combat gear laden with 168lbs of supplies and equipment. Dieppe had proved the need for absolute preparedness. What no-one knew was that the American force due to leave Weymouth, Portland and Poole in early June 1944 was to land on the bloodiest and most heavily defended beach of all – Omaha.

More than a million and a quarter of Eisenhower's Expeditionary Force were soon crowding into the south west of England, with the main element of the United States V Corps concentrated in Dorset. This consisted of the crack 1st Infantry Division ("The Big Red One"), the main components of which were its 16th, 18th and 26th Regimental Combat Teams. US Army camps sprang up in every available space with accompanying equipment and support facilities. Jeeps soon became more famil-

iar on local highways than British cars, already thin on the ground because of petrol rationing. Dorset began to resemble a vast military store of tanks, trucks, amphibious vehicles (nothing like the American DUKWs or "ducks" had ever been seen before), equipment and arms. White dust covered the hedgerows as convoys ground up road surfaces en route to the woods and fields which had been turned into huge parking lots to accommodate them, camouflaged to prevent aerial reconnaissance by the enemy. Locally encampments were made at Chickerell, Came Wood, Broadmayne, Piddlehinton, West Knighton, Bradford Down, Long Barrow and the Poundbury area of Dorchester. Hundreds more anti-aircraft guns were installed and everything possible done to conceal the colossal build-up of the invasion force. As elaborate deceptions were being put into place to convince the enemy that an assault would be made at Calais, across the shortest stretch of the English Channel, intrepid Commandos slipped ashore secretly to collect soil samples from the Normandy beaches to ensure they would withstand the weight of armour which would be passing over them.

American officers and men poured into local camps, barracks, requisitioned property and the occasional stately home. The 15th century Parnham House at Beaminster, after having been used as a military hospital, became a base for the 16th Infantry Regiment, with officers billeted in the house and men in tented accommodation in the grounds. Langton House, a 19th century Palladian mansion near Blandford became the Headquarters of the 1st Division. During its occupation the house was visited by General Eisenhower and Field Marshal Montgomery, and troops were entertained by comedian Bob Hope. Minor conversions were made to Kingston Maurward House, near Dorchester, when it was used to accommodate officers. The men were again camped in the grounds. Weymouth's Corfe Hill House and Nottington House, both empty at the outbreak of war and requisitioned by the War Department, were used as billets by the US Army, as were many houses along the Dorchester Road at Redlands. The trees surrounding Nottington House were so lush during early summer that they provided the perfect camouflage for the convoys of military vehicles converging on the area.

The population of Dorset looked on with bewilderment and not a little apprehension.

"The trouble with the GI's is – they're over-paid,

Jeeps being loaded onto landing craft at Castletown shortly before D-Day.

'Duplex Drive' or 'Swimming Tanks' being loaded at Portland after being converted to travel both at sea and on land. Tragically, they were launched in rough seas too far off-shore at Omaha to reach dry land, and most were swamped or lost in the ensuing bombardment.

American troops board LCAs in Weymouth Harbour before being taken out to the larger ships that would carry them across the Channel.

Landing craft training in Weymouth Bay before D-Day, with the town and Esplanade in the background.

Above: Portland Hard, Castletown, as the loading for D-Day continues and the invasion fleet gathers in the background.

Left: An historic but poor-quality photograph showing bulky barrage balloons lying in front of the Pavilion before D-Day, with landing craft being loaded in the background.

American troops on Weymouth Esplanade prior to boarding for D-Day.

Large infantry landing ships carried the smaller assault craft from Weymouth Bay to the Normandy beaches. Some were purpose-built, others converted passenger or cargo ships. The assault craft were slung from davits in place of lifeboats, as shown here.

over-fed, over-sexed, and over here!" went the many music hall jokes. And certainly there were mixed feelings among the residents of Weymouth and Portland as growing numbers of American troops settled into camps or billets during 1943.

"I hated 'em" remembers a Weymouth man — a teenager during the war years. "I wasn't bad looking, but as soon as the Yanks arrived I didn't get a look in with the girls!".

"They were all so gorgeous!" recalls Dawn Gould — then Dawn Yardy — who was a sixteen year old at the time. "It seemed as though the whole world had come to Weymouth!".

Corporal Bob Shipman was one of the 1st Infantry Division, battle weary beyond their years, who disembarked from a troop ship at Liverpool Docks, having taken part in the punishing North African Invasion and the capture of Sicily. Still caked in yellow mud from the Sicilian slopes, they were transported by train to points south. They had no idea where they were going, and didn't care — they were just glad to be away from the cutting edge of the war for a short time.

On his first day in camp Bob of "F" Company, 18th Infantry Regiment, was told he could go by truck into a town called Weymouth — which everybody told him was the centre of nightlife and entertainment!

The Americans could not help but be shocked at the hardships which the local people had been resigned to for the past three years. Shortages of even the most basic of foods and requirements, blackouts, the constant threat of air attack, and the ruins of bomb-blasted Chapelhay looming over the town made the newcomers feel a little guilty at the abundant supply of tinned fruit, chocolate, and cigarettes available to them.

The locals, so used to eking out their rations to the last crumb, were horrified at what seemed to them to be the off-hand wastefulness of the Americans. Peggy Lewis — now Peggy Stewkesbury — who as a teenager helped her parents run Way's Cafe in Easton Square, remembers, "They would light up and just smoke a third of a cigarette (our boys would smoke right down to the butt end) and leave a pack on the table with three or four cigarettes still inside!"

And even more galling,

"They would punch a hole in a tin of fruit, drink the juice, and throw the tin away — and we couldn't even *get* tinned fruit!".

Although they seemed to have money to burn, they were equally generous with their supplies, giving away chewing gum, Life Savers (similar to fruit Polos), O'Henry Bars, or often a tin of fruit. If the legendary handing out of nylon stockings to the girls is part of wartime folklore, it did not happen in south Dorset ; the Postal Exchanges, known as "the PX" — fixed price supplies shops set up for GIs by the US Government — were only based in major cities.

With their abundance of money and luxuries, in their immaculate uniforms in which even the lowest ranks looked like officers, caps tilted to the back of the head or low over the eyes, the local female population could not help but be dazzled by these gum-chewing, wolf-whistling young men whose like they had only seen at the pictures.

"The local lads just couldn't compete" remembers one Weymouth man. "The Yanks had it all — glamour, looks and money!"

The presence of the American forces in the area brought changes in small as well as far reaching ways. The aroma of Lucky Strikes, Chesterfields, and Camels replaced the smell of Players and Weights. Music seemed to accompany the Americans wherever they were. The lively sound of Johnnie Kerr presenting the latest hits — like 'Opus One' or 'Juke Box Saturday Nite' — on AFN radio drowned the more staid BBC Light Programme.

"They brought us Glenn Miller and Jitterbugging" remembers Mary Blackwell, who was to become a GI bride. "I was taught to jitterbug by a soldier from Georgia — I could never be thrown over the shoulder, but a lot of the girls could do it".

Dawn Yardy went one better. She was the daughter of a dancing teacher and not one to miss out on any of the techniques, but being too tall to be picked up by most of her dancing partners she would lift and swing *them* over her shoulder! Dawn and her best partner — a US Marine — went on to win a Jitterbug Contest at the Astoria Dance Hall in Tottenham Court Road, London, in early 1944.

At the almost nightly dances at the Regent Dance Hall or the Pier Bandstand, dancing styles were to change irrevocably. Peggy Lewis was intrigued by the American version of the quickstep —

"They would do the long side steps when dancing to "American Patrol", going down on one knee at the end!".

The casual clothes sported by the Americans often caused raised eyebrows. A local girl was startled

The Americans arrive.

when she first saw US sailors (known as 'Gobs') sauntering around in their off-duty apparel –

"Denim trousers, now known as jeans, brightly checked lumberjack shirts, little white hats perched on the back of their heads. They looked outrageous compared to the drab clothes we had got used to wearing".

Clothes had been rationed in England since June 1941 and the "Utility" Regulations had pared down those which were available on coupons to the severest of styles without ornamentation.

The majority of the Americans were unfailingly polite and courteous, going out of their way to give a good impression. Local people were encouraged to show hospitality to the young men, and the visitors – ever conscious that there was barely enough to go round – would appreciate being invited to Sunday tea with local families. Realising that 'coffee' in wartime Britain was either bottled Camp essence or BEV, they quickly got used to drinking tea.

"I *liked* tea", protests Bob Shipman, "but anything was better than English coffee!".

Many of the young GI's could not believe their luck when they found they were legally allowed to drink alcohol: back home this was banned to all under 21 years of age. Their determination to make up for lost time was the cause of many scraps and often sparked the constant friction between the black and white Americans.

Local pubs were the main source of entertainment for the Americans until their own club opened. One Weymouthian recalled "Inert bodies thrown into trucks by outsize American MP's after enthusiastic carousels . . .", although it has to be remembered that most local people only saw the GI's when they were off duty and "hell-bent on having a good time"!

About 10% of the Americans arriving in Britain were black and the local people (most of whom had never seen a black man before) readily accepted them and had no intention of treating them any differently, but this was resented by some of the hot-headed young whites, particularly those from the southern states, and segregation of black and white servicemen was enforced by the US military authorities. The blacks themselves were at first reserved and held back from making friends with the local people. Peggy Lewis could not help but notice.

"A black would not enter the cafe if whites were

already there. Often they would leave without finishing a meal if whites came in." When she expressed concern to an American Sergeant, he told her : "You English are giving them too much rope. You've got to let them know their place, or we'll have a Civil War when we get home".

Nevertheless, many local girls found the blacks friendly and fascinating and this would often provoke vicious riots. Eric Westmacott, whose farmer father was a mobile Special Policeman, remembers the night when a black soldier was killed in a violent fight which spilled out into the street at Lodmoor Hill, leaving puddles of blood in the gutters.

Blacks were billeted all around the Easton area in shops, houses, the Jubilee Hall, the Chapel Hall and the YMCA at Reforne. A local remembers,

"The NCO's were all educated men. One Sergeant billeted at the Jubilee Hall was a lawyer. Another played in the Count Basie Band".

But when tempers ran high and riots broke out, the blacks poured out of their billets, making whooping noises and banging their steel helmets on the ground. The US Military Police (nicknamed "Snowdrops" because of their white helmets), who regularly patrolled Easton Square, would be brought up in jeeps, four at a time, truncheons at the ready.

On Portland the black units, under white officers, were used mainly for stevedoring operations, but those billeted at Easton were known as "the Smoke Screen Gang". Their Matador lorries would daily wake the residents as they rolled down the hill to operate their smoke-generating machines which concealed the Harbour from enemy planes. "The noise they made going out from the Jubilee Hall was unbelievable – it was as if every time they went out they gave their lorries a complete overhaul or took a jeep to pieces!"

In January 1944 the burned-out Hawkes Freeman building in St Thomas Street was transformed into the US Forces Club, run by the American Red Cross with the help of local volunteers. Open from 8.30 am to 11 pm, the Club contained a dining room and dormitories, and provided the members with a tailor and shoe-shine boy! Only members of the US Forces and their guests were admitted, and local girls had to provide references from a JP and a clergyman before they were allowed to attend dances. This was a frequent venue for the First Division Band with whom Bob Shipman played trombone, and his fiancee Mary Sutcliffe would often have to sit hidden behind the drummer during non-civilian functions.

Dawn Yardy found herself in trouble at one Club dance:

"I was told off for wearing the kind of skirt that flared out when I danced. I had to wear a tighter fitting one after that!".

The same month the local Council bowed to pressure and allowed Sunday afternoon cinema opening, since wartime entertainment facilities for the vastly increased population were still decidedly limited.

Despite the fact that American Officers gave talks at the Technical College to local girls – warning them that normal life in the United States was not as it was portrayed in the Hollywood movies – many of them went on to become "GI Brides", making successful and enduring marriages.

Meanwhile preparations for the invasion accelerated. At Weymouth Harbour facilities were needed for the personnel and landing craft of the invasion force. By 1943 the shore-based HMS *Bee* controlled the Pier, the Alexandra Gardens Theatre (the base's lecture hall) and the berths along the harbourside from the Pier down as far as the Town Bridge. Since its commissioning in 1942 HMS *Bee* had served as a working-up base for coastal forces, but in October 1943 it was decided to relocate the

establishment and into the vacated areas came another shore establishment – HMS *Grasshopper* – to prepare for D-Day.

On 1st May 1944 the United States Navy Advanced Amphibious Base (USNAAB) was formally commissioned, operating the Portland hards at Castletown and taking over *Grasshopper* which then became USS *Grasshopper*. Additional buildings, used to accommodate almost 900 officers and men, included the Royal Hotel and houses and hotels in Pulteney and Clarence Buildings. Scores of houses, garages and other premises were to be requisitioned in the following weeks.

Meanwhile British services continued to be responsible for the defence of the area. The Royal Artillery manned anti-aircraft guns at coastal defence batteries at the Nothe, Blacknor, East Weares, the Breakwater forts and along the Chesil Bank, and British soldiers were accommodated at the Nothe Barracks, the Verne Citadel, and hutted accommodation among the quarries atop Portland. The RAF was in charge of signals and communications with stations at Verne Yeates and Ringstead, and many RAF men were billeted in houses at Fortuneswell. RAF rescue launches continued to operate out of Weymouth Harbour. The Royal Navy controlled the day-to-day operation of

A 'waterproofed' Armoured Fighting Vehicle on trials in Weymouth Bay, with the beach defences visible in the background.

Portland Naval Base and minesweepers, motor torpedo boats, and convoy escort ships moved constantly in and out of the Harbour.

Portland was also involved in experiments in the waterproofing of armoured cars to be driven ashore from landing craft. Exercises involving Canadian troops were carried out at Studland, and there were many "Scam" projects to test invasion techniques in and around the waters of Weymouth Bay, some presumably not providing very reliable results since the waters of the bay were often calm and flat and not ideal for simulating open beach conditions.

Sections of the "Mulberry Harbours" were tested off Osmington. The Mulberries were one of the great success stories of the invasion. To sustain an army the size of the planned landing force, the Americans and British knew that they must be able to land some 6000 tons of supplies and equipment every day on "the far shore". They could not take the risk of not immediately capturing one of the heavily-defended French ports and so they took their own "instant harbours", codenamed "Mulberries", with them.

A workforce of 20,000 men and practically the whole of Britain's concrete production went into making some 200 enormous hollow caissons, known as "Phoenix" units, which were to be towed across the Channel and sunk on site to form breakwaters a mile long. Adjacent floating piers ("whales") with connecting floating roadways enabled supplies to be unloaded and driven straight from ship

In early 1944 armoured cars were landed from LCTs into four feet of water off Weymouth Beach to test their efficiency in water. They were supposed to remain there for two minutes before driving onto the Sands.

Components of the Mulberry Harbours were tested off the Dorset coast. Those seen here are moored alongside Bincleaves Breakwater.

to shore. Additional crescent-shaped breakwaters called "Gooseberries" were made by sailing merchant ships across and scuttling them in place on arrival. Three miles out, floating steel "Bombardons" protected the whole lot from the worst of the Channel weather. Although the Americans' Mulberry was disabled in storms shortly after D-Day, the British self-assembly harbour at Arromanches was a brilliant success – parts of it can still be seen there today. After the war ended ten Phoenix units were brought back to Portland to provide destroyer berthing facilities. Two of these huge caissons (they are about five storeys high) remain there today.

Landing craft production was stepped up – Eisenhower delayed the invasion date a number of times because he felt there were not enough. By early 1944 the Hamworthy Boatyards of Bolson & Son were working day and night to turn out one complete assault landing craft a day, which were then hidden in inlets and creeks along the Dorset and Hampshire coast.

The 474th Fighter Group of the United States Army Air Force moved into Warmwell Aerodrome and the extraordinary outline of their twin-engined Lightning fighter bombers was soon to become a familiar sight in the skies above the area. Nicknamed "The Fork-Tailed Devils" by the Germans, they made many successful combat patrols over northern France and were able to return with valuable photographic evidence of enemy shore defences.

In the spring of 1944 it had become obvious to the locals that Weymouth and Portland were to provide one of the major departure points for forces taking part in the liberation of Western Europe. They could not, though, have imagined the sheer size of the operation or its impact on the area as the build-up went on.

Landmarks were removed and roads improved or widened to make way for the convoys of jeeps, trucks and armoured vehicles. Dorchester Road became a military road, and most of the residents – by now reduced to travelling by foot or cycle – were in constant danger from the increasing volume of military traffic! Bridges over rivers and railways were tested to ensure they could bear the weight of the seemingly endless deafening convoys.

Security was tightened. No-one was allowed into the area without very good reason. Only non-residents with legitimate excuses for staying were allowed to remain after midnight on 1st April 1944. On a lighter note the management of the Golden

Spring 1944 and pre-invasion security tightens.

Lion Hotel in St Edmund Street appealed for the return of the gilded tail of their ornamental lion (believed to have gone back to camp with an American serviceman in the way that local bicycles left outside pubs were wont to do – they were usually brought back the next morning).

The U.S Army Construction Corps was engaged in strengthening road access to Portland where tanks, armoured vehicles and jeeps were to be loaded for departure prior to D-Day.

The only road to the Island was over the vulnerable Ferry Bridge. In case this vital link was damaged by enemy action, a second road was constructed from Portland Road via Hillbourne Road across the fields of Downclose (now the housing estate) to the junction of Sandsfoot railway embankment, then running alongside the track to the Smallmouth railway bridge – which was modified to take road traffic – finally joining up with the main road along the causeway. It never became necessary to use this route, part of which can still be found today. The Construction Corps had also built R1 and R3 Hards – sloping concreted ramps at Castletown where landing craft could drop their bow ramps allowing vehicles to drive straight on to the vessels.

A flat marshalling area (now the Chesil Beach Car Park) was laid between the causeway and the Chesil Bank and it was here that vehicle convoys were ultimately assembled for loading onto landing craft at Portland.

In April it was confirmed that the initial assault force – United States Force 'O' – would use Weymouth and Portland as their main embarkation points for Omaha Beach. The 1st Division would spearhead the invasion, reinforced by the 115th Infantry and 116th Regimental Combat Team from the 29th Division, the 7th and 111th Field Artillery Battalions, the 741st Tank Battalion, the 81st Chemical Battalion, and the 2nd and 5th Rangers who were to take the German batteries at Point du Hoc to the west of the beach. Force 'O' numbered 34,142 men and 3,306 vehicles.

The V Corps follow-up force, Force "B", would be loaded and ready to move. The 29th Division, which included the 26th Regimental Combat Team detached from the 1st Division, totalled 25,117 men and 4,429 vehicles. They would leave Cornwall to arrive off the assault beach on the afternoon of D-Day. Scheduled to arrive on D+1 and D+2 were the 17,500 men and 2,300 vehicles of the 2nd Division, and between D+2 and D+15 a further 27 residual groups comprising 32,000 troops and 9,446 vehicles would complete the transfer of V Corps to Normandy.

Assault training was carried out in secret, and the streets and clubs would often be emptied for several days at a time while the troops of the 1st Division took part in exercises involving marksmanship, street fighting, anti-aircraft and amphibious warfare, simulated landings, destruction of beach defences, and pillbox attack.

Exercise Tiger

Two full scale landing rehearsals were planned at Slapton Sands in Devon for Assault Forces 'O' (codenamed Exercise Fabius) and Devon-based 'U' (codenamed Exercise Tiger). Slapton Sands in the South Hams was part of a 25-mile square area requisitioned for training American forces and its entire civilian population had been evacuated at the end of 1943. The terrain was similar to the beaches of Normandy.

Exercise Tiger simulated a real invasion and involved in part a fully laden convoy of eight Tank Landing Ships. These LST's moved out into the Channel from Plymouth and Brixham and were to travel approximately the same distance to the shore as if they were landing on the beaches of France. Tiger convoy T-4 of five LSTs – 515, 496, 511, 531 and 58 – left Plymouth on the morning of 27 April 1944 and was joined by 499, 289 and 507 out of Brixham. On their arrival at Slapton it was intended that their bow doors would open, ramps slam down and men and vehicles would storm up the beach to unman the defences.

T-4 never made it to Slapton. Unbeknown to those commanding the operation, the first error had already occurred in what was to become a disaster off the Dorset coast which left more than 700 Americans dead and many wounded. First World War veteran destroyer HMS *Scimitar* had been detailed to escort the LST convoy, with the corvette HMS *Azalea*. *Scimitar* had been slightly damaged in a collision the previous day and although her captain expected to continue escort duty, he was ordered to remain in Plymouth for repairs. The detention of *Scimitar* remained unreported. T-4 moved into the Channel escorted only by the armed corvette. The LSTs were armed but they were essentially slow-moving workhorses and relied on escort vessels for protection.

At Cherbourg, nine fast and menacing German E-Boats prepared to slip out into their favourite night hunting-ground, Lyme Bay, to see if any Allied shipping was in sight. The E-Boats struck in the early hours on April 28th, twelve miles off Portland Bill. Torpedoes sank LSTs 507 and 531, causing fires and explosions before they went down as fuel in the vehicles they carried blazed fiercely. 289 was also hit and damaged, but stayed afloat. In the ensuing confusion LSTs fired on sister ships, initially mistaking them for the enemy. Hundreds of men leapt from the burning LSTs into the sea, many dying of injuries, hypothermia, or simply the incorrect use of untried new-style lifejackets, which in many cases turned their wearers face-down in the water. By this time *Scimitar's* absence had been notified and HMS *Saladin* was despatched to the convoy, arriving too late to do anything more than pick up survivors and collect the dead. Blacknor Fort on the west side of Portland had been informed and could see the blazing ships but was unable to fire for fear of increasing the American casualties.

The whole invasion plan was now put at risk. The sea was littered with bodies and four of the LSTs zigzagged for the shelter of Chesil Cove. Many local people could not fail to be aware that an important operation had gone wrong, but all those who collected the drowned and brought the injured ashore were sworn to secrecy, as were the LST crews themselves and the entire staffs of the hospitals at Blandford and Sherborne where the wounded were taken. Even more serious was the fact that a small number of those on board the convoy had been issued with the final D-Day assault plan and it was vital to ascertain that they had died or been brought ashore: a prisoner in German hands could have wrecked the entire invasion. All were identified, no prisoners had been taken and absolute secrecy was maintained.

The dead were laid out at Castletown Pier. Portland-based minesweeper HMS *Sutton's* seaboat went out time after time on the grim errand of collecting bodies of American servicemen from the sea. They were taken away and even today some mystery remains as to where they were eventually buried. The rest of Exercise Tiger continued at Slapton Sands: the entire operation was a ragged performance.

Despite the setback, Exercise Fabius went ahead a few days later. Again, it was designed to simulate as closely as possible the conditions which could be expected on D-Day, carrying troops and equipment on landing craft for a distance equivalent to that from Weymouth to Normandy, and using live ammunition over the heads of and immediately in front of the troops. Unaware that they were merely taking part in an exercise and having been crammed into LSTs for several hours, the troops assumed that this was the real thing and that the beach at Slapton was in fact Omaha. Their comments on being told that it was a "rehearsal" are unreported, but can be imagined!

Intelligence showed that the Germans had concluded that any invasion of France would be via the shortest route across the Channel from the south east coast of England to Calais. The allies were determined to foster this assumption in the hope that the enemy would amass their forces to the east of the Seine, and employed all kinds of trickery to divert their attention. Along the Kent coast large numbers of wooden dummy assault craft and inflatable mock tanks were moved in to give the impression of a huge force of vehicles and equipment being marshalled for an invasion attempt.

Exercises carried out along the Hampshire coast confirmed that strips of reflective paper dropped from aircraft appeared as large air and sea forces on German radar. This technique, codenamed "Window", would be used in conjunction with simulators carried on motor launches which by transmitting radar echoes would give the impression on enemy airborne radar of a substantial sea convoy travelling up Channel towards the Calais coast, away from the intended invasion area. Persistent attacks made on enemy coastal radar installations from Denmark to the Atlantic coast of France were deliberately scattered so that the invasion sector would not be revealed by concentration on one area.

Countdown

Meanwhile, ships, landing craft and assault vessels continued to assemble in Weymouth and Portland Harbours and out in the Bay for "Operation Neptune", the codename given to the vast armada fleet massing in the ports along the Sussex, Hampshire, Dorset, Devon and Cornwall coasts. As one local man remembers:

"The number of vessels was of such a proportion you felt you could walk out to the Breakwater across the decks!"

A substantial anti-aircraft force, augmenting the existing defences, was positioned on sites overlooking the harbours. Smoke making machines continued to create smoke screens to conceal the flotilla during air raid warnings.

A top secret VIP visit took place on the 25th May when King George VI — accompanied by top ranking officers of the Royal and United States Navies — inspected the assault craft in Portland Harbour. The party had lunch on the USS *Ancon* — the Staff Headquarters Ship of the American Assault Forces — then boarded a US motor torpedo boat to inspect the vast armada. Those who might have seen the convoy of staff cars with motor cycle escorts would only find out after the event that their monarch had been in the area. "Overlord"'s Commanders, Eisenhower and Montgomery, had also toured camps and embarkation points in Southern England encouraging their assault forces to victory.

The streets of Weymouth and Portland and all available space had become a huge vehicle parking area with tanks, trucks, and armoured vehicles nose to tail along all access roads, and jeeps darting in and out of the convoys. Civilian movement was almost impossible. One local man recalls: "We had never seen so much traffic all at one time — we just had to get out of the way!"

Two photographs of the last air raid of the war on Weymouth, with D-Day only a week away. The top photograph shows Weymouth and District Hospital, the lower one Melcombe Avenue: note the telephone engineer repairing the lines.

An unexploded bomb in Melcombe Avenue, close to the route soon to be used by US troops heading for their embarkation points. Fortunately the bomb was successfully defused.

Mary Blackwell can remember, "It took two hours to get in from Upwey on the bus".

It seemed impossible that the Germans could not be aware of the massive sprawl of warships and fighting vehicles concentrated in the area. The local people lived in constant fear of an all-out air attack.

Enemy aircraft had carried out bombing raids in late April and early May, but their presence was so quickly detected that they were immediately il-luminated by searchlights – every anti-aircraft gun both in and out of range opening up on them before they were able to cause damage or injury. One man who witnessed the scene reflects :

"The barrage of fire they received was so intense that raiders aborted any idea of attack and turned back across the Channel. If they had continued with the attack they would certainly not have survived."

They did return, however – slipping through under cover of returning RAF bombers – to carry out what was to be the area's last air raid of the war. In the very early hours of the 28th May, thirty German aircraft scattered fifteen bombs over Weymouth and Portland. In Weymouth, 400 houses and the Weymouth & District Hospital were damaged, and three Civil Defence Volunteers and an ATS Commander lost their lives. An unexploded bomb was buried 28ft underground in Melcombe Avenue, and it was several days before it could be reached and defused. The bomb's presence was a cause for some concern, since it lay close to Dorchester Road, soon due to carry an endless procession of invasion-day troops and vehicles heading for the embarkation points. In the mean-time patients from the fire-damaged Hospital were evacuated by the US Army Medical Corps to Weymouth College, where an emergency hospital had been set up.

American troops based at the large 1st Divi-sion Camp at Broadmayne heard the sound of Weymouth under attack and saw the sky illuminated with bomb flashes and gunfire. Many of them had friends and girlfriends in the town, and Bob Shipman, whose fiancee was by this time his wife, remembers: "As soon as the raid was over, there was a rush to the telephone to check everyone was all right".

In Portland Harbour, the raiders laid mines among the assembled assault vessels and some twenty landing craft were damaged by the explosions. The Harbour was temporarily closed to shipping so that minesweepers could clear the area before loading was resumed.

That same day – the 28th May – the men of Force 'O' were sealed into their final marshalling camps. D-Day was planned for the 5th June, and Weymouth and Portland had become a gigantic em-barkation point for the most complex and crucial operation in history.

SIX

D-Day

For the inhabitants of Weymouth and Portland on the 1st June 1944 everyday life was a thing of the past. All aspects of their day to day existence were given over to the demands of the gigantic invasion machine, which Winston Churchill described as "Much the greatest thing we have ever attempted".

So intense was the activity, that the locals knew D-Day must be imminent. By now all contact with troops or sailors was impossible and any attempt to approach or speak to them was quickly prevented by the Military Police.

Weymouth man Royal Engineers Lieutenant John Stone, home on special leave, watched the operations – knowing he was probably the only person apart from top ranking officers who knew the destination of the mighty task force. Only days previously he had been there on a top secret mission – and the information brought back by his party had caused the timing of the whole Operation Overlord to be changed.

When volunteers for an assignment were called for, John Stone – just back from the Middle East – thought it would be a safe, local job but instead found himself in one of four groups carrying out night-time reconnaissance along the coast of France to identify mines attached to new beach defences which had shown up on aerial photographs. After two weeks of training with the Royal Marine Commandos, John Stone together with a sergeant and a corporal, faces blackened and carrying morphine tablets in case of capture, crept ashore five miles east of the proposed landing beaches to within 40 yards of patrolling sentries. They were able to identify the mines as non-magnetic anti-tank, which – had the invasion taken place as intended at high tide – would have sunk the landing craft before they reached the beach. These intricate beach defences were Rommel's design. Sent by Hitler to inspect the Normandy coast he had been shocked by the inadequacy of the fortifications and had increased the gun emplacements and added hundreds of ingenious mines atop posts on the beaches, which became known as "Rommel's asparagus".

On their return the party was interviewed by General Montgomery and later by General Eisenhower's Chief of Staff. They were the only party to return with the information. John Stone was to rejoin his Corps of the 51st Highland Division on D + 12, and was later awarded the Military Cross.

Portlander Herbert "Boy" Male, a RNVR Lieutenant, was based at Plymouth with Q57 Squadron when he was detached to Portland to skipper LCT 628 under the command of the US

A rare aerial reconnaissance photograph of coastal defences in northern France just weeks before the invasion. The type of mined beach defences visible in the photograph became known as 'Rommel's Asparagus'.

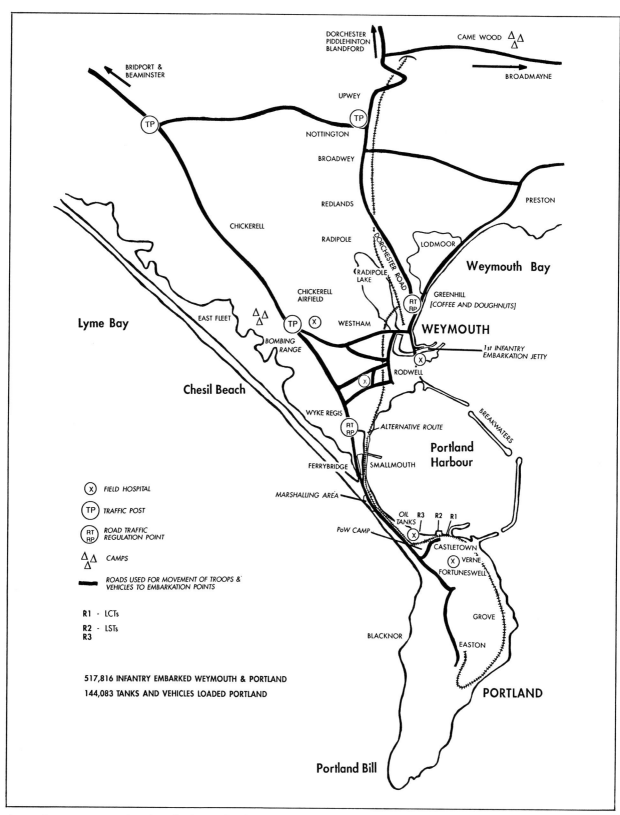

A map showing Weymouth and Portland immediately prior to D-Day.

Above: By the early summer of 1944 summer shows at the Pavilion and a stroll through the ornate gateway onto Weymouth Pier were only a memory: the whole area had become a military zone.

Below: The segregation of black and white in the American forces is clearly shown in this photograph of black 'static' troops loading rations onto landing craft in Weymouth Harbour at the end of May 1944.

The last day of May 1944 and an American Army DUKW moves onto an LST (Landing Ship, Tank). The vehicles were popularly known as 'Ducks', and owed their original name to a chance combination of manufacturer's code letters indicating the type of vehicle, date etc.

Navy to transport assault vehicles and their crews on D-Day. On the journey to Portland to join Force "O", LCT 628 was forced into Dartmouth with mechanical trouble and with a new engine fitted made the onward journey across Lyme Bay unescorted just three days before D-Day. Had she been attacked by E-boats her two 1" calibre Oerlikon guns would have been no match for the German pom-poms and the entire invasion plan could have been thrown open to the enemy – LCT

628 carried on board full instructions for Operation Overlord. Boy Male reflects "I still wake up in a sweat about that even now"!

The loading of supplies and ammunition onto the ships and landing craft continued at a furious pace, and over 500 vessels were berthed and loaded in Weymouth and Portland prior to departure for the invasion. The convoys of armoured vehicles started their journey, rumbling through Weymouth and Wyke Regis to their marshalling area on the

American Rangers on Weymouth Quay keeping fit prior to D-Day. Moored alongside are their LSI's (Landing Ship, Infantry).

causeway road, before being assembled into craft loads at Castletown and reversed into the open jaws of the landing vessels. Each loading took half an hour.

LCT 628 was loaded with 80-ton General Grant tanks, each one chained and bolted into position for the crossing.

Peggy Lewis remembers standing at the Cenotaph at the top of Portland: "There were the convoys, thick as ants, moving along the beach road, and the new hard standing packed with vehicles".

The US troops were brought in by trucks from their outlying camps to Greenhill, where they were given coffee and doughnuts before boarding their LCT's in Weymouth Harbour.

As 20-year old Mary Blackwell of Chelmsford Street got off a bus at the King's Statue at 7.30 am on the morning of the 3rd June after her nursing night shift at Portwey Hospital she saw the troops marching along the seafront towards the

Above: What has become an almost classic photograph showing American troops jauntily making their way along Weymouth Esplanade to embark at the Pier. The photograph was taken before D-Day: those who left later were more subdued.

Opposite page top: On what is now Chesil Beach car park, a line of DUKWs await embarkation in Portland Harbour.

Opposite page bottom: American Rangers prior to embarking for the initial assault on Omaha Beach. The American Red Cross supplied a traditional snack of coffee and doughnuts to each of them at Greenhill before they moved on to the embarkation point.

FROM THE FOL...CH
HOME THROUG...
AMERICAN RED...

First Lieutenant Robert T Edlin makes history as the first American soldier to board a landing craft at Weymouth Harbour for the invasion of 'Fortress Europe'.

The claustrophobic conditions inside a landing craft are well-illustrated as American troops load in the Harbour.

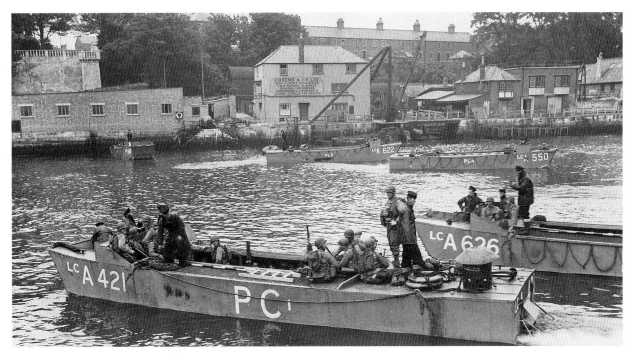

Assault landing craft move out of Weymouth Harbour to join the larger craft which will carry them across the Channel for the invasion.

Following pages: Weymouth Harbour, June 1st 1944.

Harbour. Her future husband, Platoon Leader Sgt Ken Weyrauch, was in the 1st Division's 16th Infantry Regiment, and Mary had had no contact with him since his unit had been sealed into Chickerell Camp a week before. The marching troops were all in combat dress and she was unable to recognise faces, but from over the coils of barbed wire one of the GI's called, "There's Mary!" whereupon they all cheerfully took up the call "Hey Mary! Hi Mary!". Knowing she would be one of the last of the civilian population to see them leave, she waved back enthusiastically but was hustled away by the Military Police.

As the men of the invasion force were loaded into the cavernous sweating interiors of the landing craft, their ears rang with the message from the Supreme Commander, General Eisenhower:

"You are about to embark upon the great crusade toward which we have striven these many months. The eyes of the world are upon you".

It was a cruel irony that this vast fighting force should on the 4th June face defeat by what the locals knew to be not untypical British summertime weather! The Channel, cold and grey, heaved under a blustery Force 5 westerly wind. The forecast for Normandy was one of low cloud and high seas. At 05.15 hours a 24-hour postponement was ordered. Part of Force "U" had already started out from Devon when the signal was received, and was brought into Weymouth Bay to shelter overnight and await new orders, swelling the already sizeable fleet of Force 'O' by a further 200 vessels. To this day the question of whether it was providence, a divine intervention or merely the local weather which prevented the Germans mounting an air attack on the combined forces that night remains unanswered!

The Germans had indeed relaxed their guard, believing that an invasion would not be attempted in such adverse weather conditions. In fact an invasion was thought to be so unlikely that Rommel had returned to Berlin to be with his wife on her birthday!

In the early hours of the 5th June, knowing that the combination of dawn and the tide would not again be favourable for at least another two weeks, and that a further postponement would destroy morale and risk the success of the operation, Eisenhower at his gale-lashed headquarters in Portsmouth, took the agonising decision that D-Day would be Tuesday the 6th June.

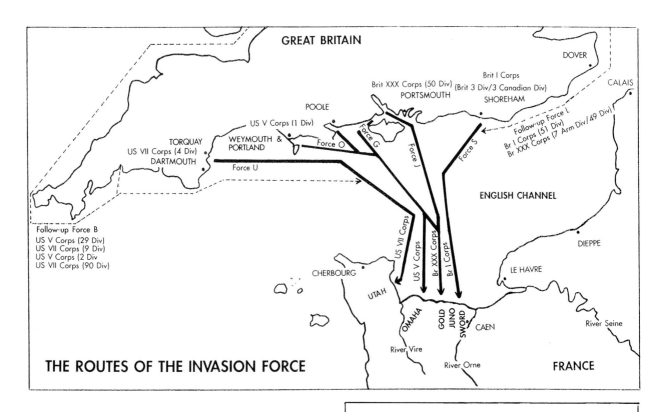

THE ROUTES OF THE INVASION FORCE

Map labels:

GREAT BRITAIN

DOVER

CALAIS

Brit I Corps
Brit XXX Corps (50 Div)
(Brit 3 Div/3 Canadian Div)
PORTSMOUTH
SHOREHAM

POOLE

US V Corps (1 Div)

Follow-up Force L
Br I Corps (51 Div)
Br XXX Corps (7 Arm Div/49 Div)

TORQUAY
US VII Corps (4 Div)
DARTMOUTH

WEYMOUTH & PORTLAND

Force O

Force G

Force J

Force S

Force U

ENGLISH CHANNEL

DIEPPE

Follow-up Force B
US V Corps (29 Div)
US VII Corps (9 Div)
US V Corps (2 Div)
US VII Corps (90 Div)

US VII Corps

US V Corps

Br XXX Corps

Br I Corps

CHERBOURG

LE HAVRE

UTAH

OMAHA

GOLD

JUNO

SWORD

CAEN

River Seine

River Vire

River Orne

FRANCE

The Armada sails

By daylight on Monday, the mighty armada had begun to ease out of Portland and Weymouth harbours bound for the rendezvous point south of the Isle of Wight; the landing craft weighted down with tanks and armoury, and the troops still huddled into the vessels where they had been for at least 24 hours – cold, cramped, seasick and scared.

An area of the Channel from St Catherine's Point to the Normandy Coast had been swept clear of mines. As the fleets from Weymouth and Portland joined with those from Devonport, Poole, Southampton, Portsmouth and Shoreham they altered course for Normandy.

That evening the only assault craft remaining in the harbours were the speedy motor torpedo boats due to depart for France in the early hours.

The sky on the night of the 5th June vibrated with the continuous roar and winking lights of thousands of aircraft passing over the south coast en route for Normandy to drop paratroops behind enemy lines and bomb German coastal defences in advance of the invasion forces. Bombers, troop carriers, aircraft towing gliders filled the sky as far as the eye could

General Eisenhower's message was issued to every serviceman who embarked for the Normandy beaches.

A loaded LST (Landing Ship, Tank) pulls away from Castletown Pier, Portland. The end of the pier was tapered down to enable the ship's ramp to connect with it, and two LSTs could be loaded at once. The Salvation Army building is clearly visible beyond the pier and in the background is the Royal Naval Hospital.

Troops aboard a landing craft in mid-Channel.

Infantry Landing Ships leave Weymouth Bay and head for the open sea. The barrage balloons, attached to the ships by cables, prevented low-flying aircraft strafing the convoy.

see, like an endless glittering conveyor belt, for hour upon hour.

John Butcher, on Home Guard duty at the railway bridge at Smallmouth remembers clearly: "At the time we did not know the significance of it — but when we looked up and saw the mass of Halifaxes and Dakotas flying over, we knew the invasion was on".

Eric Westmacott recalls: "From 2 or 3 am the planes started overhead — the sky was thick with them. The noise went on until daylight and into the morning".

Dorothy King, the Commandant of the BW Club for HM Forces in Weymouth, noted in her diary:

"Morning of June 6th: . . . From before 3 am planes started roaring overhead and they are still over now at 4.10 am. Someone is having a bad time."

And indeed they were. When the ramps slammed down at Omaha Beach at H-Hour that morning, the first men out and running through the bullet-lashed shallows had last seen land at the quaysides of Weymouth and Portland. Force 'O' — seasick and wet — was to encounter the fiercest fighting of the invasion.

The low cloud meant that pre-invasion bombing of enemy batteries had not been total. As the waves of landing craft came within range of the codenamed areas — Dog Green, Dog White, Dog Red, Easy

D-Day, June 6th 1944. Assault landing craft of the first wave of the attack pass USS *Augusta* towards the Easy Green and Easy Red sectors of Omaha Beach.

Green, Easy Red and Fox Green – they were met by a bombardment of anti-tank and machine gun fire from emplacements embedded into the 100 ft hill beyond the five mile stretch of beach. Unknown to the invasion force, the German defence was bolstered by their 352nd Infantry Division, brought up from St Lo on manouevres just days earlier.

In rough seas, the assault craft, vehicles and men of the first wave, trapped among the deadly underwater obstacles, were ripped apart by mines and merciless gunfire before they could reach the shore, and their meticulously planned tactics fell with them.

Artillery back-up failed. Twenty-nine "Duplex Drive" Sherman tanks, modified to travel through water or on land, were launched too far out and all but five were engulfed by sea and explosion.

As the landing craft moved back and forth between ships and chaotic shore carrying wave upon wave of back-up troops, the gunfire of the mighty battleships USS *Texas* and *Arkansas* blasted over

The writer Ernest Hemingway (right) sailed from Weymouth as a war correspondent on June 5th 1944. On the left is the photographer Robert Capa who sailed from Portland: of the many irreplaceable shots he took on D-Day, all but eight were accidentally destroyed during processing. Capa's driver is in the centre.

Above: A remarkable photograph of American troops taking part in the second wave of the initial assault on the Easy Red sector of Omaha Beach waiting for the ramp to be dropped.

Below: 'Bloody Omaha'. The legendary 'longest day' was for many American troops the shortest day of their young lives. It took 2,200 killed and wounded to capture a beach-head about a mile deep and three miles wide by the evening of June 6th.

their heads to destroy the formidable enemy coastal batteries.

The writer Ernest Hemingway was among the in-going assault troops who incredulously watched the battleships – vast fire-breathing monsters: "There would be a flash like a blast furnace from the 14" guns that would lick far out from the ship. . .. that sounded as though they were throwing whole railway trains across the sky".

Local man Austin Prosser was a First Lieutenant in the Royal Naval Volunteers Reserves on HMLCT 1171 which took six Sherman tanks, two half-track ammunition lorries and two half-track ambulances into Omaha Beach.

"It can only be described as chaotic and alarming. We arrived at the spot where we had been told to unload, but the beach was littered with wrecked assault craft and wounded or dead Americans. The beachmaster was desperately looking for engineers to blow a way through so the troops could get off the beach. We were caught in crossfire from the bunkers at each end of the beach. We laid off while a destroyer sailed from one end to the other firing its guns to try to destroy the gun emplacements. About 10 o'clock, after going in and pulling some broken down assault craft off the beach and removing some bodies, we landed our load. As far as I can recall very few of the tanks we landed ever got off the beach."

The eldest crew member on HMLCT 1171 was its 22-year old skipper.

For the famous war photographer Robert Capa there was no joy in returning to his native Europe. As he threw himself from the landing craft onto Easy Red in a hail of bullets he described it as "the ugliest beach in the whole world". Filming with shaking hands, he said later :

"The foreground of my pictures was filled with wet boots and green faces. Above the boots and faces, my picture frames were filled with shrapnel smoke ; burnt tanks and sinking barges formed my background".

Capa made it back to an LCI and began helping to transfer the wounded from the shore. Six hours after leaving the USS *Chase* he was back on board, just as the last wave of troops in landing craft were being lowered for their assault. He could not bring himself to return to the beaches and stayed on board. The decks by this time were ". . . already full with returning dead and wounded . . . The mess boys who had served our coffee in white jackets and with white gloves at three in the morning were covered with blood and were sewing the dead in white sacks".

When Corporal John McComas of A Company, 26th Regiment, landed with back-up Force "B" that afternoon he was set down in water above his head. Swimming ashore he found the shallows tinted red with the blood of his countrymen: "We were

Accurate fire from German shore defences narrowly misses the USS *Arkansas* off Omaha Beach.

Above: A photograph taken by Lt. 'Boy' Male on D-Day. British LCT 628 offloads an American General Grant tank on Omaha Beach.

Below: June 9th 1944. A German prisoner is settled onto a stretcher by American medics. Captain Harold Thomas noted on the back of the photograph, 'A Jerry prisoner – quite happy'.

A remarkably serene Omaha Beach a few days after D-Day.
German prisoners can be seen behind the tent on the right,
awaiting shipment back to Weymouth and Portland.

moving among the bodies of dead men to escape the enemy fire. Our own guns were too wet to shoot".

Despite the devastation on the shoreline and the relentless mortar and artillery shelling, the invasion somehow seemed to be inching forward. The experience and courage of the men of the First Division was paying off, and by the evening small groups had broken through the inner beach defences and were gaining the heights beyond.

Colonel George Taylor, Commander of the 16th Infantry Regiment, leading men through dead and wounded colleagues towards gaps in the obstacles, yelled, "Two kinds of people are staying on this beach, the dead and those who are going to die – now let's get the hell out of here!"

By nightfall, the beachhead had been won and some 3,000 troops of V Corps had been killed, wounded or were missing.

Ken Weyrauch was left for dead on Omaha Beach. His squad was blasted apart by German shelling and all but three were killed. ·The next day, shell-shocked, speechless, and barely alive he was picked up by medics and evacuated.

About D + 17. On board LCT 628 after the three-day storm which devastated the Mulberry Harbour and caused havoc on the invasion beaches. In the background a destroyer and some smaller vessels can be seen washed ashore on the sand bars of Omaha Beach.

Back to Base

Back in Weymouth and Portland, the gunfire glowed red across the Channel as the locals waited for news.

Within 24 hours, ships and landing craft began to slip back into Portland Harbour to unload the wounded and re-load with back-up troops and supplies.

The outgoing infantry — almost passing the return-ing casualties as they left — were less jaunty and cheerful as they marched along the Esplanade. The locals would quietly watch them — this time with subdued sadness. It was now known what lay in store for them on the beaches of "Bloody Omaha".

Dorothy King from her home in Brunswick Ter-race, noted: "9 am, June 7th 1944: Thousands of men waiting at this moment in front of the house resting . . . Civilians are not allowed to speak to any

American officers use a German fortified bunker as a temporary office.

or cross the road".

The *Dorset Daily Echo* on the 6th June reported: "Communique No 1 set the world agog today. It was issued from Supreme Headquarters, Allied Expeditionary Force (SHAEF for short) at 9.33 am and said – 'Under the command of General Eisenhower, Allied naval forces, supported by strong armies, began landing Allied armies this morning on the northern coast of France'."

The US Army Field Hospitals which had been set up across the area were suddenly packed with the returning wounded. The volume of traffic in the Channel between the beaches and Portland meant that it was D+6 when Ken Weyrauch reached the 50th Field Hospital near Connaught House. Gangrene had set into his left arm, which was immediately amputated. Ken survived his severe injuries and married Weymouth girl Mary Blackwell before being flown back to America to recuperate. Fifty years later, shrapnel from the blast is still working its way out!

For the first seven days LCT628 ran a shuttle transporting tanks from ships to the shoreline, "hauling that blasted tank door up several times a day".

As the invasion of France progressed, Weymouth and Portland continued to send thousands of men and assault vehicles to Normandy, and LCT's would chug back and forth between the harbours and Omaha Beach – a 300 mile round trip exposed to south westerly winds, mines, U and E-Boats, and aerial attack. Just one week after D-Day the British destroyer HMS *Boadicea* was sunk by a Junkers torpedo-carrying bomber off Portland with the loss of more than 170 men, and the frigate *Blackwood* was torpedoed by a German submarine two days later.

Late June saw allied troops preparing to capture Cherbourg, and a task force of battleships and destroyers left Portland on the 25th June to bombard enemy defences around the vital port area. The cruiser HMS *Glasgow* was hit by enemy shells and

Left: June 7th or 8th. German prisoners of war are landed by US Coastguards at R3 Hard on Portland.

Below: German prisoners marching into Victoria Square, Portland. They are on their way to a transit camp set up on the Royal Navy officers' sports ground off Cadets Road. The Masonic Hall in the background was used as an American Forces Club called 'The Doughnut Dug-out'. The convoy of Sherman tanks is headed for Castletown to be loaded onto LSTs or LCTs.

Right: A poster for the last of the tremendous Savings Weeks which took place throughout the war. 'Salute the Soldier' week on Portland appropriately took place in the month following the D-day landings.

PORTLAND
SALUTE THE SOLDIER
WEEK

JULY 15—22

OUR TARGET:
£25,000
For a Complete Medical Unit

He Is Gaining HIS OBJECTIVE In Normandy

HOW TO SAVE:
SAVINGS STAMPS 8d., 2/6 and 5/-
NATIONAL SAVINGS CERTIFICATES
15/- each, worth 20/6 in ten years
DEPOSITS IN POST OFFICE and
TRUSTEE SAVINGS BANKS
3% DEFENCE BONDS in units of £5
upwards. Interest half-yearly
3¼% NATIONAL WAR BONDS 1952-54
3% SAVINGS BONDS 1965-70

AND WHERE:
Banks, Stockbrokers, Post Office, Trustee
Savings Banks, Selling Centres or your
Savings Group

 # WE MUST REACH OURS!

FULL WEEK'S PROGRAMME OF EVENTS

SATURDAY, JULY 15th
3 p.m.—OFFICIAL OPENING CEREMONY at the War Memorial (if wet in the Drill Hall) by the Minister of Food, the Rt. Hon. Colonel J. J. Llewellin, M.C., M.P., accompanied by Lord Hinchingbrooke, M.P. There will be a Parade representative of all H.M. Forces, Civil Defence, and other organisations, with the Bands of the Dorset Regiment and another famous Regiment.
7.30—"FLASH." A Revue at the Borstal Club.
7.30—"HAPPY-GO-LUCKY." A Revue at the Drill Hall, presented by Sergt. Bex. of an R.A. Regiment.

SUNDAY, JULY 16th
3.00—MUSIC in Victoria Gardens. Dorset Regimental Band.
7.45—SPECIAL SERVICE at the War Memorial.

MONDAY, JULY 17th
8.00—DANCE at the Portland Borstal Club.

TUESDAY, JULY 18th
6.30—MUSIC in Easton Square. Dorset Regt. Band.
7.00—SOCIAL in the British Legion Hall.
7.30—ORGAN and VOCAL RECITAL at St. John's Church.
8.00—SOCIAL at Portland Borstal Club.

WEDNESDAY, JULY 19th
2.30—CHILDREN'S SPORTS at Tophill School Playing Field.
7.00—WHIST DRIVE at First-Aid Hut, Easton Lane.
7.30—DANCE at the Drill Hall, Band of a famous Regiment.
7.30—CINEMA SHOW at Portland Borstal Club.

THURSDAY, JULY 20th
2.45—WHIST DRIVE at British Legion Hall.
5.30—PUNCH and JUDY SHOW at Victoria Gardens.
6.45—PUNCH and JUDY SHOW at Easton Square.
7.15—WHIST DRIVE at Portland Borstal Club.

FRIDAY, JULY 21st
6.30—MUSIC in Victoria Gardens. Dorset Regt. Band.
7.30—DANCE at the Verne (open to the public). Music by Band of a famous Regiment.

SATURDAY, JULY 22nd
2.15—SPORTS MEETING at Borstal Stadium.
7.30—CONCERT PARTY by Whiteheads S. & A.C.

ALL THE WEEK—TRAIL OF PENNIES, organised by the W.V.S.
PLEASE DISPLAY YOUR FLAGS OR BUNTING
THROUGHOUT THE WEEK—
TENNIS TOURNAMENTS AT THE PORTLAND BORSTAL CLUB AND FIXED JACK COMPETITIONS AT THE EASTON BOWLING CLUB.

SALUTE THE SOLDIER
HE DOES THE FIGHTING—YOU DO THE SAVING!

This page is sponsored by
Messrs. J. A. DEVENISH & Co., Ltd.; Messrs. ELDRIDGE, POPE & Co., Ltd.; and PORTLAND NATIONAL SAVINGS COMMITTEE.

returned to Portland along with the USS *Texas*, which had an unexploded 240 mm shell embedded below decks.

From D-Day until the end of the summer of 1944, some 304,000 men and 85,000 fighting vehicles bound for Normandy were loaded on to ships and landing craft at Weymouth and Portland Harbours. Returning vessels brought over 26,000 dead and wounded British and Americans, German Prisoners of War, and civilian refugees in to the ports. Allied forces were still embarking from the area, and the wounded and the captured were being brought ashore, but the summer of 1944 saw Weymouth beginning to return to its pre-war function as a holiday town.

Mrs Dorothy King wrote in her diary: "Sunday, 16th July 1944 – Beach crowded with children and bathers – but procession of all kinds of vehicles passing all day. There are still some US soldiers here, including coloured ones, but most have now gone across".

Local establishments were put to use as emergency hospital accommodation. The Verne Citadel was used as a medical clearing centre for seemingly uninjured survivors, but it was often found that men suffering from shock or body wounds had declared themselves fit in order to avoid hospitalisation and to be returned quickly to their fighting units. The bar of the Royal Victoria Lodge Hotel in Victoria Square at Portland became a temporary emergency hospital.

The locals were once again drawn into a supportive role. Dawn Yardy was one of the Red Cross girls who were driven by truck to the cluster of US Army Hospitals near Blandford to provide chat and sympathy for the injured servicemen. On one visit she was urged by a nurse to speak to a young man – most of whose face had been blown away – and to reassure him that he was still attractive to girls.

Some 40,000 German prisoners of war were brought into Weymouth and Portland, and locals soon became used to mingling with the once feared enemy – who turned out to be ordinary fathers, husbands, brothers and sons like everyone else. The family of Weymouth farmer Eric Westmacott had two German POW's assigned to them for two years. Billeted at Martinstown, Wolfgang and Hans were brought up every day to help on the farm. Hardworking and respectful, the two became almost part of the family and corresponded with Mrs Westmacott for several years after the war. Dawn

The rusting remains of LCT A2454 still lie beneath the Chesil shingle, and are here shown during an exceptionally low tide in 1974.

Yardy was later to marry a German prisoner of war – Manfred Heinrich – a Luftwaffe pilot who had been captured on the Dutch border at the end of 1943.

Victory Assured

The allied invasion forged ahead, with Force "O" reaching St Lo in July. Paris was liberated on the 25th August. Although the euphoria of Victory celebrations was many months and several setbacks away, the news reports of Allied victories in Europe were generally encouraging. A country sick of years of air raids and austerity began to relax.

The ban on travel was lifted. August Bank Holiday visitors poured into Weymouth by bus and train, almost as if to prove that despite everything "the seaside" was still there. They flocked to the only available area of the beach and to the Pier Bandstand where the Band of the Green Howards entertained with lively music and community singing. South of the Gloucester Hotel the whole of the sands was still out of bounds, as were both piers, the Pavilion, the Alexandra Gardens and the Nothe. Most people brought their own food. There was no beer, no ice cream and seaside rock was a minty memory. Buckets and spades couldn't be bought, but a wooden spoon and a billycan did just as well.

In September the blackout restrictions were partially lifted and many local children saw street lighting for the first time in their lives. The regulations remained in force and were now known as the "dim-out". If the sirens sounded, it was to be "lights-out" again. A coastal zone extending five miles inland retained some lighting restrictions until the very end of the war.

Yet further acts of extraordinary courage were shown in mid-October when eleven lives were claimed by Portland's old adversary – the sea. On a stormy afternoon a tank landing craft was dashed ashore close to Chesil Cove, nine crewmen being instantly swept away and drowned, leaving two ratings clinging perilously to the wave-swept wheelhouse. Coastguards mounted a rescue operation but lines fired to the stricken vessel fell wide as it rolled and slewed in the forceful undercurrent. Three coastguards waded into the surf to free the line, but although colleagues on the shore managed to grab and save the life of Wyke District Officer William Rowsell, mountainous seas swept away retired Naval Commander J. A. Pennington Legh and Coastguard Robert Treadwell. Fireman George Brown then fought his way out to the vessel and after three hours battling against the waves managed to bring the two crew ashore. Already commended by the RNLI for his part in the rescue of two airmen from a D-Day aircrash three miles out at sea, he received an award at Buckingham Palace for his courage off Chesil Beach. The Portland Council Chairman paid special tribute :

"Among many deeds of self sacrificing heroism in the age old tradition of those who dwell on the beach, we would like publicly to applaud the outstanding gallantry of George Brown, a young man of this Island".

The widows of Commander Legh and Officer Treadwell received posthumous bravery awards on behalf of their late husbands. Robert Treadwell's courage had also been twice recognised – on June 28th that year he had rescued the crew of a landing craft wrecked at Whitenose.

As more and more areas of Europe were liberated by the Allies, steps were taken to arrange for the reorganisation and reconstruction of war damaged zones. The Ministry of Health urgently needed experienced medics and in December 1944 Weymouth was honoured by the fact that its Medical Officer of Health, Dr Gordon Wallace, was called to join the Civil Affairs Branch of the Army in Europe.

December – the start of what was to be the coldest winter for fifty years – saw the Home Guard officially "stood down".

There was still some activity in the Channel, however, and LST's daily left Portland Harbour for the French coast under constant threat of attack from U-Boats.

On New Year's Eve a twenty vessel convoy was torpedoed off the Bill by U772, two ships being hit, but the U-Boat received its come-uppance the following day when it was depth charged by a Wellington bomber on patrol from Chivenor, never to surface again. But February 1945 saw the sinking of the SS *Everleigh* by enemy U-Boat U1017, six men being lost and 43 survivors brought ashore at Portland.

February also brought news that the Allies had crossed the German frontier, and as winter turned to spring, coastal air protection from Warmwell was no longer thought to be necessary. 152 Squadron was withdrawn and the Aerodrome ceased to be operational in April.

British people were saddened in that month to hear of the sudden death of the American President. Winston Churchill was to say of him: "In Franklin Roosevelt there died the greatest American friend we have ever known and the greatest champion of freedom who has ever brought help and comfort from the New World to the Old".

News of another death two weeks later was, however, received with less solemnity. On the 30th April, cornered by the advancing Russians, Adolf Hitler committed suicide in his Berlin bunker. By early May, the locals were eagerly awaiting a formal announcement that the war was over.

Mrs Dorothy King of the BW Club noted in her diary, "Saturday, 5th May 1945: Germans surrendered this morning to General Montgomery ..." and on the 7th May she wrote, "Peace declared about 7.30 pm. Announced in music programme on the wireless".

VE Day was announced on the 8th May. In Weymouth some 10,000 people blocked the Esplanade outside the Gloucester Hotel to attend a thanksgiving service, which closed with a final sounding of the "All Clear".

Public transportation was free and bars, clubs and restaurants were open throughout the day and into the night. All thoughts of an ordinary working day

Author Denise Harrison's mother, then Poppy Collins, joins in the seafront celebrations on VE Day, May 8th 1945. Flags are flying and Weymouth is in a holiday mood again after five years of war.

The first U boat to surrender on the cessation of hostilities in Europe, U 249, is escorted into Weymouth on May 10th 1945. Two more followed and visitors were able to view them on paying an entrance fee which went to one of the Royal Naval charities.

were pushed aside as elation swept through the area.

"It was like Carnival Day" remembers Dawn Yardy, "Everyone was going around hugging everybody else!".

Dancing to the Bob Newsam Band at the Pier Bandstand continued well into the early hours, and the music was relayed through speakers along the Esplanade. Not confined to places of organised entertainment, dancing and general rejoicing took place in every street and home. Five years of living in fear had come to an end and on Portland an effigy of Hitler was hung from a Straits lamp post!

The consequential order for enemy vessels to sur-render brought three U-Boats into Weymouth. On the 9th May the 5 officers and 43 ratings of U249 were brought in by the frigates HMS *Magpie* and HMS *Amethyst*, followed by U1023 later the same day and U776 on the 16th May.

In May 1945, Portland received a letter of thanks from US Army Colonel Sherman L Kiser which read: " ... Through Portland hundreds of thousands of American vehicles and specially trained troops have passed over your roads, through your town, and received the hospitality of your people ... The people of Portland and its outlying districts have given the American forces the finest co-operation possible."

On the Sunday following VE Day a March Past and a Church Parade of all the local Civil Defence services was held on Weymouth Esplanade and at St Mary's Church.

So the people of Weymouth and Portland could ease themselves back into a form of ordinary life.

In five years they had lived through a turmoil of tragedies, losses, emotions, and celebrations they could never have imagined a community could endure, and had emerged proud in the knowledge that whatever fate threw at them, or whatever the exceptional circumstances demanded of them, they rose to the challenge with resourcefulness and courage.

So many people say of the war years, "Despite everything, they were good times. Everybody pulled together – everybody helped everybody else". It is a pity that the lessons learned then have now – fifty years later – been almost forgotten. Let us hope that by celebrating this fiftieth anniversary those values, which worked so well before in times of trouble, can be re-called, dusted off, and tried again.

SEVEN

Postscript 1945

It was time to take stock. More than 7,000 homes in Weymouth had been damaged in air raids. Of these more than 400 were demolished or had to be pulled down. Over 1,000 were severely damaged and the rest were in need of some repairs. At Portland, 40 houses had been destroyed and more than 300 seriously damaged.

Eighty three Weymouth civilians, including six Civil Defence personnel, had lost their lives in air raids : 37 in Portland. Countless families in the area had received news of relatives killed, wounded or missing in action.

The post-war problems facing Weymouth and Portland would be the same as at the end of World War I – unemployment and housing.

Redevelopment of the blitzed Chapelhay streets

Looking up towards the top of Chapelhay Steps in 1957 – the flats are under construction, top left. All the bombed buildings on the right were pulled down. Across the Backwater can be seen the old gas retort house (not a war casualty) which was demolished later.

was a priority, but disagreements over the plan rumbled on for years. Eventually "Chapelhay Heights" filled the site. These were Weymouth's first purpose-built flats, with commanding views over the Harbour. Below them, the war-torn streets of "Old Weymouth" were cleared in 1961 to provide a site for the Municipal Offices.

A temporary solution to the housing shortage was the erection of substantial numbers of prefabricated houses. These steel-framed, factory-built single storey homes were intended to have a 10-year lifespan, but many lasted much longer. When the first "pre-fab" was completed in Radipole Lane it was "open to the public" and 6,000 people turned up to inspect it during August 1945. Other sites were chosen, including Camp Road and Bedford Road and at Weston on Portland. Another prefabricated structure was to provide the first Public Library in Weymouth: the "temporary" prefab opened in 1948 and lasted until 1990!

King George III had been reprieved. The early months of 1944 had seen the fate of the King's Statue vying with the war news for prominence in the local press. There were serious proposals to move the monument, for reasons ranging from its being a traffic hazard to a dilapidated eyesore. Eventually it was decided to renovate the Statue and paint it green pending a final decision on the road layout in the vicinity (the Statue's present heraldic colours date from 1949 ; the large traffic island in front of it was constructed in the mid-fifties).

In 1945 the last few hundred evacuee children returned home and their "Welcome Club" in King Street closed. It had been run by the ladies of the Women's Voluntary Service, who also coped with refugees, the homeless and numerous other emergency situations as they arose. The King Street premises were shared by one of the town's British Restaurants and some of these continued for several more years, as did some food rationing.

The 27th May 1945 saw a huge Farewell Parade

Bomb damaged Franchise Street. The shops of Gordon Row now stand on the site of the old General Gordon Hotel.

Gordon Row today. Kempston Road can be seen curving uphill in the background of both pictures.

of Weymouth Civil Defence Services on the Recreation Ground in Newstead Road. It was the first anniversary of the deaths of three of their members in the last air raid on the town. Portland's stand-down parade was held on the 30th June, five years exactly since the first bomb fell in 1940 in Chesil Cove. No one realised then what a huge debt of gratitude would be owed to these brave people who had served their townsfolk so well.

During May the US military authorities relinquished all of Weymouth Beach apart from a small area at its southern end : the US base would soon be closing down. Pneumatic drills were brought in to pulverize the concrete tank traps on the seafront, and the remaining rusty barbed wire entanglements were removed. Bulldozers shifted heavy obstacles from the sea and dug out buried obstructions. The Esplanade shelters had a coat of paint, Punch and Judy returned and it was once more possible to stroll along the Nothe Walk and Stone Pier.

On June 1st Weymouth and District Hospital returned "home" after a year in temporary accommodation at Weymouth College, following the extensive air raid damage of May 1944.

June 19th saw the presentation of the colours of the United States of America by the US Navy to the Island and Royal Manor of Portland at

As service personnel left the area, the services canteens, hectically busy during the war years, became redundant and closed down. Portland's opened late in 1943 and closed in June 1946, producing this souvenir brochure to mark the event. It ends with a short poem, the last verse of which reads:

So don't forget your Canteen Night
And what you did to make life bright
For those who served on land and sea
And in the air to set us free.

The Stand Down parade of Weymouth's Civil Defence Forces on May 27th 1945 at the Newstead Road Recreation Ground (later Weymouth Football Club and now the site of a supermarket).

St John's Church, Fortuneswell. Two months later, the US Ambassador to Great Britain unveiled a tablet at Portland commemorating the momentous events of June 1944 and at the same time renamed Cadets Road, "Victory Road" in recognition of the thousands of US troops who had passed through the Island.

Demobilisation of the forces began on 18th June 1945 and gradually service men and women returned to their families. For many other families there were no joyful reunions, as news of those reported "missing in action" was confirmed as "killed in action".

Summer brought two war associated tragedies. In June a bather drowned as he stumbled into one of the deep holes left in the Bay by landing craft. These were then marked as they were found, and

later filled in. A few days earlier horrified crowds at Sandsfoot Beach had witnessed the loss of an RAF plane and its Canadian pilot when the aircraft crashed into shallow water just 50 yards offshore.

The hugely popular American Red Cross Club in St Thomas Street closed for the last time on 11th July 1945. The VE Day exploit of Sergeant David Fink was recalled: "who earned undying fame by driving his jeep straight into the hall of the Club"! Another popular services club closed in September – Mrs Dorothy King's "BW" Club at St John's Hall.

August Bank Holiday 1945 saw the town filled to overflowing. The Alexandra Gardens Theatre was back in the entertainment business, but not the Pavilion. The Theatre had been retained by the military and from October served as the Weymouth Foreign Parcels department of the GPO, handling parcels landed from Royal Navy Ships wherever they put in around Britain's coast. Although the Pavilion was de-requisitioned in January 1946, it was some time before it was re-opened under a new name – The Ritz – only to be destroyed by fire in 1954. It was summer 1946 before all the requisitioned properties, including some hotels, were handed back. Weymouth Pier did not re-open until 1st June 1946, its steamers returning from war service and refits that summer also.

There were more Victory celebrations in August 1945 when VJ (Victory Over Japan) Day was announced on the 15th and the Second World War had finally ended world-wide.

There were still plenty of reminders of war in Weymouth and Portland, the most prominent being the ugly red brick and concrete street shelters, which became a traffic hazard as road transport began to move freely again. In October a start was made in demolishing them. The first one to go, in Mitchell Street, took some shifting, a crane swinging a one-ton steel ball making little impression on it for quite a time. It was years before they were all removed, and the garden "Andersons" lasted even longer.

In November, Mayor John Goddard finally handed the Chain of Office to his successor. This popular and public-spirited man had served the town well throughout the war years. Sadly, he died in 1946 only days before he was to be granted the Freedom of the Borough.

On the stroke of midnight, 31st December 1945, HMS *Attack* at Portland ceased to exist : it was time for HMS *Osprey* to return home.

A New Year without war began.

Appendices

BUILDINGS MENTIONED IN THE TEXT BUT WHICH NO LONGER
EXIST OR HAVE CHANGED THEIR USE.

A1 Stores, Greengrocers, St Thomas Street, Weymouth. Now occupied by Comptons, Stationers.

Alexandra Gardens Theatre, Esplanade, Weymouth. Closed as a theatre in the 1960s – now an Amusements Centre.

Borstal Institution, Grove, Portland. Now Young Offenders Institute.

Breweries, Hope Square, Weymouth. John Groves and J A Devenish amalgamated in 1960 under the Devenish name. No brewing is done in Weymouth now. Buildings converted to Timewalk/Museum.

Central School, Cromwell Road, Weymouth. Became Westham Secondary School and moved site. Buildings now being demolished.

Christchurch, King Street, Weymouth. Demolished 1956-7. Garnet Court shops and flats built on the site.

Clinton Arcade/Restaurant. Top end of St Mary Street/St Thomas Street. Built 1927 on site of the Royal Baths. Arcade ran between the two main streets. Now converted to individual shops (Pizzaland, Mothercare) and arcade no longer exists.

Connaught House, Cross Road, Weymouth. 1860s mansion between Wyke Road and Buxton Road. Later a school. Emergency hospital in World War II. Demolished 1988. Houses built on site.

Edward Hotel, 16 The Esplanade, Weymouth. Converted to apartments.

Gloucester Hotel, Esplanade, Weymouth. Now converted to Gloucester Apartments and Offices.

Hawkes, Freeman, General Furnishing Store, 39 & 40 St Thomas Street, Weymouth. Now occupied by Courts Furnishings.

Holy Trinity School, Chapelhay, Weymouth. Demolished. Houses of Trinity Court fill the site. School relocated to Cross Road.

Jubilee Hall, St Thomas Street, Weymouth. Built to commemorate Queen Victoria's Golden Jubilee 1887. Converted to Regent Theatre and Dance Hall 1926. Cinema under different names and finally a Bingo Hall. Demolished 1989.

Palladium Cinema, Town Bridge, Weymouth. Closed as a cinema in 1931. Currently occupied by Steam House Cafe.

Pavilion Theatre, Weymouth Pier. Burned down (as "The Ritz") in 1954. Present Pavilion Theatre built on the site in 1960.

Pier Bandstand, Weymouth. Only the structure on the beach remains – the actual "pier" was blown up as unsafe in 1986.

Portwey Hospital, Wyke Road, Weymouth. 19th century workhouse. Emergency hospital in World War II. Post-war maternity hospital. Now apartments.

Radipole House, Fernhill Avenue, off Dorchester Road, Weymouth. Demolished. Radipole Court homes built on site.

Regal Cinema, Fortuneswell, Portland. Closed as a cinema in the early 1970s. Became a Night Club. Building burned down in 1992.

Regent Cinema and Dance Hall, St Thomas Street, Weymouth. See "Jubilee Hall".

Ritz Theatre, Weymouth Pier. Post-war name of the Pavilion Theatre. Burned down in 1954. Present Pavilion Theatre on the site.

Rodwell Station, on the Weymouth and Portland Railway. Line closed to passengers in 1952. Station platforms can still be seen between the Buxton Rd and Wyke Rd bridges which cross the old line.

Sidney Hall, bottom of Boot Hill, Weymouth. Demolished 1987. Asda store/car park now on the site.

Smallmouth Viaduct, on the Weymouth and Portland Railway. Line closed to passengers in 1952, to goods in 1965. Viaduct demolished in 1971.

South Dorset Technical College, Newstead Road, Weymouth. Now one of the two sites of the present Weymouth College, a tertiary college.

Southern Times, Weymouth. Local weekly newspaper. It ran from Victorian times until the early 1960s.

V H Bennett, Department Store, St Mary Street/St Thomas Street, Weymouth. Currently occupied by John Menzies, New Look and Quality Seconds.

Webb Major, Timber Yard, Commercial Road, Weymouth. Demolished. Now a car park between Wooperton Street and Quebec Place.

Weymouth College Boys Public School, Dorchester Road, Weymouth. 1863 – 1940. Buildings used as a Teacher Training College post-war. Now one of two sites occupied by the present Weymouth College, a tertiary college.

Whitehead's Torpedo Works, Ferrybridge, Wyke Regis. More recently Wellworthy's light engineering factory. Now owned by A E Piston Products Ltd.

Wyke Hotel, Portland Road, Wyke Regis. Renamed "Wyke Smugglers".

The list below includes air raids in the Weymouth and Portland area where bombs are known to have fallen on land: it excludes attacks on shipping and air fights.

Abbreviations: HE = High Explosive, I = Incendiary, O = Oil, UXB = Unexploded

Date	Day	Time	Bombs	Area
1940				
30 June	Sun	evening	1 UXB	Portland – Chesil Cove
4 July	Thur	0840	1 HE	Portland – Castletown
27 July	Sat	0015	6 HE	Upwey – Watery Lane
				Weymouth – Marina Gardens, Russell Avenue
11 August	Sun	1021	39 HE, 19 UXB	Portland – Castletown, Southwell
				Weymouth – Belle Vue Road, Bincleaves House, Brewery Allotments, Buxton Road, Clearmount Road, Connaught House, Franchise Street, Hope Square - both breweries, Longfield Road, Melbury Road, Newberry Gardens, Newstead Road, Old Castle Road, St Leonards Road, The Marsh, Underbarn, Wardcliffe Road, Westham Cross Roads, Wyke Road (No 102). All UXBs fell in Rodwell
15 August	Thur			Portland – Borstal Institution, Bumpers Lane
17 August	Sat	0140	5 HE, 1 UXB	Weymouth – Beaumont Avenue, Dale Avenue, Lodmoor, Weymouth Bay Avenue
18 August	Sun	0120	8 HE, 5 UXB	Weymouth – Abbotsbury Road (Ames Shop), Holland Road, Radipole House, Dorchester Road, Radipole Lake, South Dorset Technical College, Weymouth Grammar School
28 August	Wed	2158	6 O	Weymouth – Abbotsbury Road, incl "Westdowne", East Wyld Road, Lanehouse Rocks Road, Quibo Lane
4-13 Sept				Weymouth – 4 "tip and run raids". No damage
15 Sept	Sun	1400	I	Portland – Fortuneswell, St John's School
30 Sept	Mon	1656	4 HE	Weymouth – Green Lane, St David's Road
5 October	Sat	2035	3 HE	Portland – Naval Base
			I	Weymouth – Lodmoor
21 October	Mon	1215	3 HE	Weymouth – Southern National Garage, Edward Street
			1 O	Melcombe Regis Gardens
14 November	Thur	2340	6/8 HE	Weymouth – Lodmoor, Manor Road, Mount Pleasant Avenue
14-17 November				Weymouth – minor raids – no damage, Lodmoor and Redlands
17 November	Sun	2100	2 mines	Weymouth – Bincleaves Road (The Dragons), Chapelhay Street, Dorset Terrace, Franchise Street, Holy Trinity Schools (Chapelhay), North Quay, St Leonard's Road, Trinity Terrace
19 November	Tue	2000	16 HE, 2 UXB	Weymouth – Buxton Road/Connaught Road junction, Green Lane, St Martin's Road, NE of Stoke Road
30 November	Sat	1830	6 HE	Weymouth – Corfe Hill, Radipole Church, Radipole Lake, Radipole Manor, Ullswater Crescent
1941				
2 January	Thur	1849	1 HE	Portland – Harbour
			I	Weymouth – Goldcroft Road, Radipole Lane, Radipole Village

3 January	Fri	2240	3 HE	Weymouth – Abbotsbury Road/Radipole Lane junction (in a field), East Wyld Road, Harbour, Radipole Lane
16/17 Jan	Thur/Fri	2300	8 HE, I	Weymouth – Everest Road, Faircross Avenue, Preston (in fields), S of Rylands Lane, I's at Chesil Beach, Radipole and Radipole Church, nr Whitehead's Factory, Wyke, Town/Rodwell area
17/18 Jan	Fri/Sat	2144	1 HE, I	Weymouth – Weymouth Railway Station sidings. I's N of Spa Hotel, Radipole, White Horse, Osmington
4 April	Fri			Weymouth – Preston – no damage
14/15 April	Mon/Tue	night		Portland – Augusta Road, Borstal Institution, Kingsway Hotel, Queens Road
15/16 April	Tue/Wed	2145/0215	56 HE, I	Weymouth – Abbotsbury Road/Lanehouse Rocks Road junction, Argyle Terrace, Buxton Road/Rodwell Road junction, Fernhill Avenue, Goldcroft Road, Great Western Terrace, Heathwood Road, Lynch Road, Marquis of Granby, Portwey Hospital area, Radipole House, Dorchester Road, Rodwell Station, Sutcliffe Avenue.
1 May	Thur	1300	HE	Portland – Harbour
				Weymouth – Whitehead's Factory, Wyke
3 May	Sat	2230	5 HE, I	Weymouth – Ashton Road, Ferrybridge, Wyke
4/5 May	Sun/Mon	2320	13 HE	Weymouth – East Wyld Road, Norfolk Road, Shirecroft Road, Suffolk Road, Weymouth Railway Station goods yard
6/7 May	Tue/Wed	2400	HE, I, 2 UXB	Weymouth – Bincleaves Road, Cross Road, Down Road, Marina Gardens, Rodwell Road, St Leonard's Road, Wyke Road Rodwell Railway Cutting (2 UXB)
9 May	Fri	0430	5 HE	Weymouth – Holy Trinity School (trench shelters), Oakley Place
11/12 May	Sun/Mon	0018	32 HE, I	Weymouth – Everest Road allotments, Franchise Street, Goldcroft Road, Golf Links, Oakley Place, Spring Gardens, St Leonard's Road, Weymouth & Portland Railway Line, I's at Wyke and Rodwell
14/15 May	Wed/Thur	0255	1 HE	Weymouth – Sidney Hall Car Park
29 May	Thur	0240	6 HE	Weymouth – field E of Williams Avenue, Wyke
30 May	Fri	evening		Portland – House near Borstal Institution
13 July	Sun	2335	HE	Weymouth – Franchise Street, Oakley Place
11/12 October	Sat/Sun	2355/0320	HE	Portland – Harbour
				Weymouth – open land N of Wyke Rd
1 November	Sat	2320	4 HE	Weymouth – Abbotsbury Road/Perth Street junction, Abbotsbury Road/Longcroft Rd junction, Royal Adelaide PH, Southview Road, Sussex Road

1942

23 March	Mon	1953	15 HE	Portland – Naval Base, Chiswell, Underhill
				Weymouth – Castle Cove (in sea)
24 March	Tue	2115	7 HE	Weymouth – Nottington House (rear of), Preston (in fields), Radipole Lake
2 April	Thur	2150	HE	Weymouth – Buxton Road/Portland Road junction, N of Camp Road, Chickerell Flying Field, Cromwell Road, Essex Road, Glen Avenue, Golf Course, Granville Road, Greenhill, Holly Road, Knightsdale Road, Links Road, Milton Road incl Wesleyan Chapel, Newstead Road, Nicholas Street incl Fox Inn and Echo Works, Norfolk Road/Quibo Lane junction, Radipole Lane, St David's Road, Sluice Gardens, Greenhill, Sewage Works, Southlands Road, Springfield, Wyke Road (nurses' quarters)
13 April	Mon	0806	2 HE	Weymouth – Commercial Road, Granville Road
28 June	Sun		HE	Weymouth – Benville Road, Bradford Road, Chapel Lane, Upwey, Kayes Lane, Wyke, E of Marine Terrace (on beach), Shrubbery Lane incl Ship Inn, Southview Road, allotments Victoria Road, Wyke
29 June	Mon		I	Weymouth – Abbotsbury Road, Westham generally

2 July	Thur	0301	HE	Portland – Crown Farm and 50/60 other buildings
			2 UXB	Weymouth – Old Castle Road, Verne Road

1943

10 March	Wed	2100	6 HE	Portland – Alexandra Inn, Easton Lane, Grove Road
			3 HE	on open ground

1944

20 April	Thur	0030		Portland – light damage
24 April	Mon	0126	3 HE	Portland – scattered incidents
				Weymouth – Overcombe
7 May	Sun			Portland – no damage
14 May	Sun			Portland – no damage
15 May	Mon			Portland – Chesil Beach, Underhill
28 May	Sun	0101	16 HE, UXB	Portland – Harbour – mines laid, damaging LCTs of invasion fleet
				Weymouth – Lodmoor, Lynmoor Road, Melcombe Avenue incl Weymouth & District Hospital, Southill area, Wyke

APPENDIX 3

THE WAR MEMORIALS

On Sunday, 8th May 1949 a plaque was unveiled on WEYMOUTH WAR MEMORIAL on the Esplanade to commemorate the Weymouth dead of World War II. It does not list individual names. These are inscribed in *The Book of Remembrance, World Wars 1914-1918 and 1939-1945.*

The Book and its memorial stand are in St Mary's Church, Weymouth. It lists the names of those in the Borough of Weymouth and Melcombe Regis who died in both World Wars - members of HM Forces and civilians. It was dedicated by the Bishop of Sherborne on the 13th September 1950, and the pages are turned one at a time, each week.

PORTLAND WAR MEMORIAL, Yeates, Portland is inscribed with the names of the Island's dead of both World Wars.

THE AMERICAN STONE, Portland. A plaque presented to Portland by the 14th Major Port, US Army was mounted on a commemorative stone and unveiled in Victoria Gardens by the American Ambassador, John G Winant on the 22nd August 1945. At the same time he renamed "Cadets Road" at Underhill "Victory Road" as a permanent reminder of the momentous events of 1944.

THE AMERICAN MEMORIAL, Weymouth. A plaque presented to Weymouth by the 14th Major Port, US Army was mounted on a column opposite the Royal Hotel on Weymouth Esplanade. It was unveiled by Major General Clayton L Bissell, DSC, DFC, US Military and Air Attache on the 3rd December 1947. The column has a lamp on top which is lit continuously.

Curiously, on the unveiling of both American memorials the weather was blustery and the sea grey and heaving, much as on the 6th June 1944.

The American Memorial unveiling, Weymouth Esplanade, December 3rd 1947.

The inscription on Portland's American Memorial tablet.

" The Major part of the American Assault Force which landed on the shores of France on D-Day, June 6th, 1944, was launched from Portland Harbour. From June 6th, 1944 to May 7th, 1945, 418,585 troops and 144,093 vehicles embarked from this Harbour.

This plaque marks the Route which the vehicles and troops took en route to the points of embarkation.

Presented by the 14th Major Port U.S. Army.

Harold G. Miller,	Sherman L. Kiser,
Major T.C.	Colonel T.C.
Sub Port Commander.	Port Commander.

Portland's American Memorial in its present-day setting.

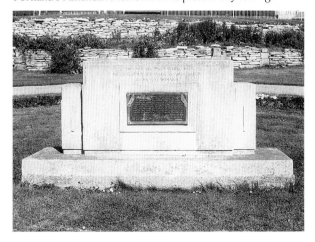

Further Reading

Numerous books have been published about the Second World War, but those which are listed below contain information of particular relevance to the Weymouth and Portland area.

Acutt, Douglas G F *Brigade in action:* the history of the development of the St John Ambulance Brigade, and of its co-operation with the Civil Defence Services during the War 1939-1945. Sherren and Son, Weymouth (1946).

Boddy, Maureen and West, Jack *Weymouth: an illustrated history.* The Dovecote Press, 1983.

Carter, Geoffrey *The Royal Navy at Portland since 1845.* Maritime Books, 1987.

Dawson, Leslie *Wings over Dorset:* Aviation's story in the South. Dorset Publishing Company, 1983.

Hill, Ron – as told to Lye, Marion *Weymouth at War:* Ron Hill's story of the vessel *My Girl.* Dorset Publishing Company, 1990.

King, Dorothy *Happy recollections.* Henry Ling, Dorchester, 1946.

Legg, Rodney *Dorset at War:* diary of WW2. 2nd edition. Dorset Publishing Company,1990.

Male, Herbert Gordon *Being in all respects ready for sea.* Janus Publishing Company, 1992.

Morris, Stuart *Portland: an illustrated history.* The Dovecote Press, 1985.

Murphy, John *Dorset at war.* Dorset Publishing Company, 1979.

Although subjected to wartime press censorship, the local newspaper files of the *Dorset Daily Echo* and the *Southern Times* for the 1930's and 1940's provide a wealth of material, as do the minute books of the Borough.

Index

Some buildings mentioned in the book have changed their use or have been demolished since World War II. Appendix 1 lists these.

Major air raids which are illustrated in the text are included in the Index : a complete list can be found in Appendix 2.

Weymouth and Portland's War Memorials are described in Appendix 3.

Illustration numbers are printed in italics.